YOUR ULTIMATE FREEDOM

HIDDEN CURSES REVEALED

Pamela A. Wood

ABBA Ministries
2220 East Irlo Bronson Memorial Hwy
Kissimmee, FL 34741
www.abbapeople.com
www.yourultimatefreedom.net

Photographer: Scott Wood
Cover design by M.H. Pasindu Lakshan
Prophetic art: Liz Camacho

Library of Congress Registration Number: TXu 2-229-809

Paperback ISBN: 978-1-7361730-0-8
E-Book ISBN: 978-1-7361730-1-5

Printed in the United States of America

DEDICATION

This book is dedicated to those reading this book who are seeking a deeper relationship with the LORD. My prayer is that every hindrance is removed, and you achieve your ultimate freedom so you can walk in a greater level of intimacy with the LORD and receive all the blessings GOD has for your life.

ACKNOWLEDGMENTS

I want to express my deepest gratitude to my husband who supported me in prayers and words of encouragement throughout the writing process. Your critiquing helped to pull the best out of me. You never gave up on me and kept encouraging me to trust that HOLY SPIRIT would give me the words needed to complete the book.

I am forever grateful to HOLY SPIRIT for depositing in me the urgency, the desire, and the anointing to write this book.

I want to express my appreciation to Apostle Nebby Gomez who prompted me to write this book. He was relentlessly encouraging me until the book was complete.

I want to express my sincere thankfulness to all who faithfully prayed for me during the process of writing this book.

TABLE OF CONTENTS

Dedication

Acknowledgments

INTRODUCTION

GOD loves us so much that He provided the ultimate sacrifice for our sins, for our healing, and our deliverance. Part of that deliverance is breaking curses off our lives. The Word of GOD specifically tells us that there are two reasons why curses come upon us. The first is if we curse Israel.

> *"I will bless those who bless you, and I will curse him who curses you; And in you, all the families of the earth shall be blessed."*
>
> *- Genesis 12:3*

If we come against Israel, the apple of GOD's eye, expect the judgment of GOD. The scripture is very clear. We need to have love toward the people of Israel. If we want the blessings of GOD in our lives, we need to speak blessing over Israel and come to her defense when needed. I believe the reason why GOD's sovereign mercy has been upon America is because of the support we have given Israel. Under certain presidencies, this relationship was tarnished. But praise GOD, we are moving in the right direction to reestablish a healthy relationship.

The second cause for curses to come upon our lives is when we do not heed to the voice of GOD and obey His commandments. GOD's Word is not a bunch of rules to keep us bound. They are prophetic instructions that bring guidance, direction, and protection to our lives. They are not difficult to understand, He gives us basic instructions through His Ten

1

Commandments. Deuteronomy 28 is very clear regarding obedience to His instructions. Blessings will come to those who obey (Vv. 1-14), and curses will come to those who do not (Vv. 15-68).

These blessings or curses can come upon individuals, cities, and even entire nations. America was once a blessed and prosperous nation because it was built upon a Judeo-Christian foundation. Over the years America has turned its back on GOD and passed laws contrary to His Word. We are to obey the laws of the land if they do not contradict GOD's Word and His commandments. Unfortunately, many Christian churches are compromising the Word of GOD by embracing immoral laws and justifying their actions through a false understanding of GOD's grace and love. Sin is not being confronted, the Word of GOD is being watered down, and society is decaying because of it. JESUS, the Messiah is the answer. Through Him, our sins can be forgiven, and curses can be broken off our lives.

GOD's love is demonstrated through sacrificing His only Son to die for our sins. We are to reciprocate that love by obeying His commandments and accepting JESUS the Messiah as our LORD and Savior. It is because of GOD's love for us that He instituted the Law. It was not established to punish us. It was established to protect us from harm and to guide us in our everyday living. JESUS refers to GOD's basic commandments in the following scripture:

> *Jesus said to him, "' You shall love the LORD your God with all your heart, with all your soul, and with all your mind'. This is the first and great commandment. And the second is like it: 'You shall love your neighbor as yourself.' On these two commandments hang all the Law and the Prophets."*
> *- Matthew 22:37-40*

If we love the LORD with all our heart, we won't serve other gods, put anything or anyone before Him, nor take His name in vain. If we love our neighbors as ourselves, we won't bear false witness against them, steal from them, nor bring any harm to them.

2

Introduction

Jesus's proclamation of these two commandments is so profound. To better understand the full depth of what He said, we must ask Holy Spirit to bring us revelation to understand the essence of each commandment. We can't look at them from just the literal sense, but we must also look at what the Spirit of the Law is saying to us as well. When we disobey God's commandments, we open the door for curses to come upon our lives. Often, we are afflicted with curses because we do not realize we are disobeying God's commandments. Removing these sins from our lives will cancel curses, bring freedom and transformation, and draw us closer to God.

This is the purpose of my book, *Your Ultimate Freedom-Hidden Curses Revealed*. The book is divided into three sections. Section 1 teaches the importance of your spiritual diet, how strongholds develop, what is deliverance, and how to obtain it.

Section 2 gives a deeper insight into God's commandments. As you study each of the ten commandments through the revelation of Holy Spirit, you will have a better understanding of how you offend the heart of God and unnoticeably open doors to curses upon your life. Each chapter is filled with testimonies of those who have gained the revelation, repented of their sins, broken curses off their lives, and are now walking in the blessings of the Lord. All names have been changed to protect the identity of the individuals and/or family members of the individuals.

Section 3 contains a list of underlying spirits that may be in operation luring you to walk in disobedience and break God's commandments. It also includes prayer guides that can be used for ministering deliverance. *Your Ultimate Freedom-Hidden Curses Revealed* can be used in a home church setting for teaching purposes and it also serves as a guideline for ministering deliverance. This is only a tool. Allow Holy Spirit to guide you as you seek your deliverance or assist others in achieving theirs.

In His love,
Pam Wood

SECTION 1

THE DELIVERANCE PROCESS

Chapter 1

HOW IS YOUR DIET?

When you hear the word diet what comes to your mind? For most, it is the act of restricting certain foods while emphasizing others. In other words, a list of dos and don'ts. There are many types of special diets: the grapefruit diet, the Keto diet, the Atkin's diet, the low-fat diet. The list can go on and on. Some individuals will even go on a crash diet to lose weight rapidly over a short time. Does any of this sound familiar? If you are one of those individuals who have viewed dieting in this way, you have probably lost the weight you wanted, only to gain it back and much more once you went back to your old eating habits. Most diets to lose weight will have you consuming certain foods and eliminating others. These types of diets are unbalanced and may not give you all the essential nutrients needed to keep your body healthy. That is why you need to transform your way of thinking and see dieting as a healthy approach to eating. It is a lifelong eating plan that involves making healthy food choices every day. A healthy diet will provide the nine essential nutrients needed to function properly. Diets are temporary and if you want to keep the excess weight off, it requires radical lifestyle changes.

The same concept is true for deliverance. If you view GOD's Word as a bunch of laws restricting you from certain activities and requiring you to perform others, you will eventually stop following the Word of GOD. If you focus on just the New Testament and deprive yourself of the spiritual nutrients of the

Old Testament, or only focus on scriptures that make you feel good, you will become spiritually malnourished. You cannot approach deliverance as a "quick fix" and expect lasting results. Sin is the root of your spiritual heaviness. That is why the author warns you in the book of Hebrews to lay aside every weight, and the sin which so easily ensnares you.

> *Therefore, we also, since we are surrounded by so great a cloud of witnesses, let us lay aside every weight and the sin which so easily ensnares us, and let us run with endurance the race that is set before us.*
>
> *- Hebrews 12:1*

Are you carrying excess weight?

If an athlete is carrying excess weight, that individual will not perform to his or her potential. The same applies to your spiritual life. Sin will weigh you down and it will be difficult to run with endurance, some may even quit the race because of their bondage with sin. Sin opens the door for your body, mind, and soul to come under demonic influence. The only way to get rid of the excess spiritual weight is to repent and go through a process of deliverance. Deliverance is not a quick fix. It is a daily sanctification process where you allow yourself to be transformed by the power of HOLY SPIRIT. Just as crash diets have a temporary effect on a person's life, quick-fix deliverances are only temporary as well. The Word of GOD gives a clear warning of this.

> *"When an unclean spirit goes out of a man, he goes through dry places, seeking rest; and finding none, he says, 'I will return to my house from which I came.' And when he comes, he finds it swept and put in order. Then he goes and takes with him seven other spirits more wicked than himself, and they enter and dwell there, and the last state of that man is worse than the first."*
>
> *- Luke 11: 24-26*

If you continue to be conformed to this world and do not allow HOLY SPIRIT to transform your mind and deliver you from your sins, you will be worse off than before. I have witnessed this myself. People will come for deliverance and in time go back to their old ways of living. They end up more tormented and miserable than they were before they started the process of deliverance. It is only through a daily walk with HOLY SPIRIT that you take off the spiritual heaviness that weighs you down and keeps you from having intimacy with GOD. See the Word of GOD as a book of lifelong instructions that will provide you with the necessary tools to transform your life into the image of Christ. If you follow His basic instructions, you can walk in freedom and live a victorious life.

How is your spiritual weight? Do you feel a heaviness or oppression over your life? Are you spiritually dehydrated? Through the power of HOLY SPIRIT, you can be set free from the bondage of your sins. The remaining chapters in the book can guide you in the right direction and bring the revelation you need to remove that heaviness so you can live a life of freedom. As you read each chapter, eat of the spiritual food set before you and watch the weight of sin come off.

Questions for Thought

1. How do you keep excess spiritual weight off?
2. What will happen if you view GOD's Word as a list of dos and don'ts?
3. How can you become spiritually malnourished?
4. What will be the results if you approach deliverance as a quick fix?
5. What steps do you need to take to maintain your deliverance?

Chapter 2
WHAT'S ON YOUR MIND?

Have you ever had a thought come to your mind which was totally out of character and wonder, "Where did that come from?" I think all of us can say this has happened. But what you do with those thoughts can make a huge impact on how you think and feel.

Your mind is a huge battlefield. The enemy of your soul, Satan, will try to fill your mind with impure thoughts, negative thinking, and take you down a whirlwind of destruction. He knows your weaknesses and will do everything in his power to torment you and try to make you doubt the reality of GOD's love for your life. A thought may seem harmless, but it can become physically, emotionally, or spiritually dangerous. That is why you must take every thought captive and compare it to what the Word of GOD says. If it does not line up to GOD's Word, get rid of it. Do not entertain the lies of the enemy. Doing so will open a door for the enemy to bring torment to your life.

> *For as he thinks in his heart, so is he.*
>
> *- Proverbs 23:7*

What controls your actions?

Your thinking determines the way you feel and how you feel determines your actions. That is why the enemy tries to bombard your mind with impure thoughts, doubts, and fears. As you entertain those thoughts, your emotions and actions respond accordingly. You will not be able to control your actions if you do not control your thoughts. The Book of Proverbs gives the warning to guard your heart. The heart guides the choices you make and the actions you choose.

> *Keep your heart with all diligence, for out of it springs the issues of life.*
> - *Proverbs 4:23*

> *"But those things which proceed out of the mouth come from the heart, and they defile a man. For out of the heart proceed evil thoughts, murders, adulteries, fornications, thefts, false witness, blasphemies."*
> - *Matthew 15:18-19*

If you allow your emotions to gain the upper hand, you will respond by taking some sort of action. Your thoughts influence your emotions and physical reactions. You react according to how you think and feel. If the enemy continues to nag you with unholy thoughts and you allow your emotions to respond to those thoughts, it will produce negative actions. Those negative actions will then form bad habits and before you know it, a demonic stronghold has you bound. The existence of a stronghold can be recognized because it will be that area of your life in which you consistently have problems and cannot live in victory.

> *For those who live according to the flesh set their minds on the things of the flesh, but those who live according to the Spirit, the things of the Spirit.*
> - *Romans 8:5*

The following scenario happens quite often and can easily be avoided if individuals can understand how strongholds develop.

Manuel was a married man and had a fabulous job. Although he loved his wife, there were many problems within the marriage. He found it easier to focus on his career rather than resolving his marital issues. One day as he was working at his desk, he noticed a beautiful co-worker walk by. Throughout the day he kept thinking about how beautiful she was. For days he could not get the thoughts of her out of his mind. A few days later he arrived to work and as he entered the building, this same attractive woman arrived at the same time. Manuel opened the door for her, and they greeted one another and exchanged names. Again, he was drawn to her attractiveness. Weeks later he went into the breakroom and saw Allison sitting at a table having her coffee break. The aroma of her perfume attracted him, and he invited himself to share his coffee break with her. He sat down and began a conversation with her. He started flirting with her and she responded positively. Within minutes he placed his hand on her hand and told her how beautiful she was.

From day one Manuel should have rebuked the thoughts of this attractive woman, but he didn't. He had opened a door to sin, entertained the attractiveness of the woman, and he allowed lust to enter his heart. This happened long before sitting down with Allison in the breakroom.

> *"But I say to you that whoever looks at a woman to lust for her has already committed adultery with her in his heart."*
> *- Matthew 5:28*

If you entertain thoughts like these, they will open doors to temptation. That compromise in the breakroom led to a full-blown affair. Manuel knew what he was doing was wrong, but he could not overcome his fleshly desires for Allison. For months he tried to break off the relationship but to no avail. A stronghold of sexual immorality and adultery took root in his life. Unfortunately, this extramarital affair destroyed his marriage.

What is your weakness?

You may say, "I don't struggle with sexual immorality." That may not be your weakness, but there are many others to consider. Do you constantly struggle with rejection or insecurity? When something doesn't go your way, do you respond with anger?

"Timothy shared with me for years he struggled with having a bad temper. If someone cut him off in traffic he would manifest with anger. It didn't take much to set him off. Once he had an argument with his wife and out of anger, flipped the table and it ended up landing on his toe. He had to go to the emergency room for stitches. HOLY SPIRIT grabbed hold of his life, he received the help he needed, got delivered from a spirit of anger, and now is living a victorious life. Every time he looks at his toe, the scar reminds him of how strong that spirit of anger was in his life. He is thankful that the enemy no longer has the victory over him."

Never accept the lie of Satan that you are the way you are and can never change. Your past does not have to define your present. JESUS died on the cross for your sins and can give you the power to overcome every demonic stronghold that keeps you bound. Receive your freedom today!

Questions for Thought

1. Why is it important to guard your heart?
2. How can you guard your heart?
3. How do strongholds form?
4. How can you prevent strongholds from forming in your life?

Chapter 3

WHY DO I STRUGGLE?

Is there an area of your life that is a constant struggle? It might be something as simple as a bad temper or lying. Maybe you struggle with depression or addiction. You have prayed, fasted, and cried out to the LORD to remove this from your life. You find relief for a short time, but then it returns, and you find yourself back in the same battle. If this sounds like you, you are not alone. This is how Satan wants you to live. His tactics are to keep you bound and not experience the freedom GOD has for your life.

Can a Christian have demons?

If I were to ask a Christian if they believed that a demon can reside in the life of a believer, most would say no. Some would even say demons do not exist. Others will ask, "How can HOLY SPIRIT and a demon dwell in the same place?" Some believe if you are demonized before coming to JESUS then you are automatically set free from demons when HOLY SPIRIT comes into your life. Are any of these your way of thinking? These deceptions are lies that Satan uses to stop Christians from seeking the deliverance they desperately need.

I believe part of the confusion is when a person is told they have a demon, they mistakenly think we are saying they are demon-possessed. This is not the case. To be demon-possessed implies that Satan owns you. As a believer, Satan does not own you, you belong to JESUS. But Christians can be attacked mentally, emotionally, and physically because of curses or open doors from sin in their lives or from their generational lines. These open doors give Satan legal rights to attack. Many Christians genuinely love the LORD but are unable to overcome certain strongholds of their lives.

"William openly admitted his struggle with pornography and sexual fantasies. Even though HOLY SPIRIT brought conviction of sin, he could not overcome his addiction nor receive the victory he so desperately desired. Fortunately, his desperation to be free superseded any shame he was feeling and, was able to openly confess his sin. He openly spoke to his father and his father admitted that he had committed adultery years ago and that his father too fell into the same sin. Thank the LORD, through deliverance and canceling an iniquity of sexual immorality in his family's generational line, William was set free. That was several years ago and to this day he has not fallen back into any sexual temptations."

Don't allow shame or guilt to keep you from seeking help. This is a trap of the enemy to keep you bound and stop you from receiving total freedom. If you are one who does not understand or is perplexed about whether a Christian can be influenced by demons, I trust the Word of GOD will bring clarity to the confusion of this topic.

> *Do you not know that you are the temple of God and that the Spirit of God dwells in you?*
>
> *- 1 Corinthians 3:16*

We are the temple of GOD and HOLY SPIRIT dwells within us. The moment we accept JESUS as our personal Savior, we receive HOLY SPIRIT, and our spirit receives new life. The adversary receives an eviction and HOLY SPIRIT fills our spirit with His presence.

In the Old Testament, we know that people went to a physical place to enter the presence of GOD. The Old Testament tabernacle of GOD consists of three parts: the outer court, the inner court, and the Holy of Holies. The entire tabernacle signifies the presence of GOD, but the actual place where GOD dwelt was in the Holy of Holies.

How is the temple of GOD constructed today?

Now may the God of peace Himself sanctify you completely; and may your whole spirit, soul, and body be preserved blameless at the coming of our Lord Jesus Christ.
- 1 Thessalonians 5:23

Just as the Old Testament tabernacle was made up of three parts, your earthly temple is also. It is comprised of a spirit, soul, and body. Your body represents the outer court, your soul represents the inner court, and your spirit represents the Holy of Holies. Each must be thoroughly sanctified so the enemy can't accuse you and you can stand blameless before GOD. If one of these areas is not sanctified, then the work of the cross is not complete, and you will not have the total peace that GOD has for your life.

It is important to understand that HOLY SPIRIT resides in our spirits, otherwise we would seek HOLY SPIRIT based on how we feel or from our own way of thinking. Salvation is a spiritual event where our spirit becomes alive through YESHUA, JESUS Christ. The spirit represents the eternal part of our being. It is owned by either Satan, the ruler of this world, or by GOD. When you receive JESUS Christ as your personal Savior, you become a child of GOD.

But as many as received Him, to them He gave the right to become children of God, to those who believe in His name.
- John 1:12

*The Spirit Himself bears witness with our spirit that we are
children of God, and if children, then heirs--heirs of God and
joint-heirs with Christ, if indeed we suffer with Him, that we
may also be glorified together.*

- *Romans 8:16-17*

As a sinner, you are redeemed by His grace and through the
blood of JESUS. As a believer of JESUS, you are GOD's inheritance.
The more you allow the power of HOLY SPIRIT to sanctify your
life, the more Christ-like you become. Through this purification
process, you will reflect the glory of GOD in your life and inherit
eternal life.

*"And I give them eternal life, and they shall never perish;
neither shall anyone snatch them out of My hand."*

- *John 10:28*

The moment you accept JESUS as your personal Savior, the
enemy is given an eviction notice and HOLY SPIRIT fills your spirit.
Your spirit now belongs to GOD and no one can snatch you out of
His hand. The Greek translation for snatch is *harpazo* which
means to siege or take by force[1].

*Now He who establishes us with you in Christ and has
anointed us is God, who also has sealed us and given us the
Spirit in our hearts as a guarantee.*

- *2 Corinthians 1:21*

*And do not grieve the Holy Spirit of God, by whom you were
sealed for the day of redemption.*

- *Ephesians 4:30*

According to these two verses, when you establish a covenant
relationship with JESUS, your spirit is sealed. If you stay in
covenant with GOD, Satan cannot touch your spirit, you are
protected by the hands of GOD. Satan cannot forcefully pull you
out of His hands. However, this does not give you the right to

think that you can do whatever you want. Many think that once saved, always saved. You can willingly give up your inheritance and remove yourself from GOD's hands if you knowingly sin and allow the influences of Satan to have dominion over your life. The Word tells us to expect the judgment of GOD.

> *For if we sin willfully after we have received the knowledge of the truth, there no longer remains a sacrifice for sins, but a certain fearful expectation of judgment and fiery indignation which will devour the adversaries.*
>
> *- Hebrews 10:26-27*

Where does Satan attack?

A demon cannot enter your spirit and reside where HOLY SPIRIT resides. However, nothing prevents Satan from attacking your body and soul. It is here that you face your daily decisions of allowing HOLY SPIRIT to control your thoughts and actions or live under the influence of sin. Satan's influence in your life is often hidden and controlled through various strongholds. I will address how demonic strongholds develop in the next chapter. Strongholds can be in the form of demonic oppression and can manifest in various degrees of torment. That is why many Christians are bound and cannot live a victorious life.

> *For if you live according to the flesh you will die; but if by the Spirit you put to death the deeds of the body, you will live.*
>
> *- Romans 8:13*

The soul consists of our mind, will, and emotions. It is here where you face daily decisions of spirit-controlled living or allowing the desires of the flesh to control your thoughts and emotions. That is why part of the armor of GOD is the helmet of salvation. The enemy, Satan, loves to attack the mind of believers and bring torment. Apply the blood of JESUS over your mind, asking for protection from evil thoughts and lies from the enemy. If a thought comes that is not from GOD, rebuke it and command it to leave. If not, you entertain the thoughts of the enemy and fall victim to his traps. Don't allow your thoughts to take you down a path of destruction.

Could your health be an indicator of something deeper?

The Bible teaches that the richness of our soul has a direct correlation to our health. Many times, we seek to find the cause of our physical ailment without considering the possibility of a spiritual root.

> *Beloved, I pray that you may prosper in all things and be in health, just as your soul prospers.*
>
> *- 3 John 1:2*

Your health could be an indicator of what the condition of your soul is. Have you been praying for healing and have not yet received it? Ask the LORD to show you if there is any unforgiveness, anger, or resentment in your heart. These things can prevent your prayers from being answered. In the Book of Luke JESUS heals the paralytic through the forgiveness of his sins.

> *"When He saw their faith, He said to him, "Man, your sins are forgiven you."*
>
> *- Luke 5:20*

In verse 24 of the same chapter, JESUS tells the paralytic to rise, take his bed, and go home. Through the forgiveness of sin, this paralytic was healed. John 5 gives another account of this paralytic. In this account JESUS gives this warning:

> *Afterward, Jesus found him in the temple, and said to him, "Sin no more, lest a worse thing come upon you."*
>
> *- John 5:14*

From these two, scriptures you can see there is a connection between sin and sickness. Why are so many tormented with sickness? Could there be a root of sin in their lives and that their souls need deliverance! If you are in ill-health, ask the LORD to show you if there is any root causing the sickness.

Have you checked your emotions lately?

"Be angry, and do not sin": do not let the sun go down on your wrath nor give place to the devil.
- Ephesians 4:26-27

Apostle Paul gives warning not to allow your emotions to be an open door for the enemy. In the above scripture you can see that when you sin, it allows the devil to torment you. Sin opens the door to demonic influences in your life. Anger is a powerful stronghold that can open the door to spirits of resentment, hatred, rage, and even cause one to kill.

Whoever hates his brother is a murderer, and you know that no murderer has eternal life abiding in him.
- 1 John 3:15

"But those things which proceed out of the mouth come from the heart, and they defile a man. For out of the heart proceed evil thoughts, murders, adulteries, fornications, thefts, false witness, blasphemies."
- Matthew 15:18-19

The Greek translation for heart used in this scripture is *kardia* which figuratively means the thoughts or feelings (mind)[2]. The Complete Jewish Bible version brings a better understanding to this scripture.

"But what comes out of your mouth is actually coming from your heart, and that is what makes a person unclean. For out of the heart come forth wicked thoughts, murder, adultery and other kinds of sexual immorality, theft lies, slanders."
- Matthew 15:18-19 (CJB)

Is it a slip of the tongue?

Have you ever had someone say something to you that was very hurtful? I have heard people say "Oops, I'm sorry, I didn't mean to say that." According to scripture, that which is spoken has come from within a person's heart. Sometimes you say things out of anger or frustration and try to justify it as being a slip of the tongue. When this happens, search your heart.

For as he thinks in his heart, so is he.

- Proverbs 23:7

What is the root of your sickness?

Worldly doctors are now supporting the truth found in GOD's Word. A study conducted by John Hopkins School of Medicine found that individuals who became quickly angered were three times more likely to develop premature heart disease and five times more likely to have an early heart attack.[3] I know of someone who was a very negative, critical individual who had difficulty controlling his anger and constantly put people down.

"Andrew was the type of individual who could only see the worst in people. He constantly complained and never had anything good to say about himself or other individuals. He also had difficulty controlling his anger. Anything would set him off. In his early 60's he suffered a heart attack and had to have open-heart surgery. He made it through surgery but the day after the surgery his heart stopped beating for a short amount of time. The nurses did not perform CPR on him because he had a living will and did not want to be resuscitated. Fortunately, his heart started beating after a minute.

Some said to him, "Maybe GOD isn't ready for you yet." He knew this was not the case. The LORD strongly spoke to Andrew and gave him names of specific individuals that he needed to go and ask forgiveness for things he had done to them. He followed through and asked for forgiveness from specific individuals. Fortunately, the LORD gave him a chance to make things right with these individuals and transform the condition of his heart before slipping into eternity. A year later Andrew died and went to be with the LORD."

You can see from the testimony above that the open door to sickness was a sin. The physical ailment of his heart was a direct manifestation of the condition of his spiritual heart. The only way your soul can be sanctified and preserved blameless is to surrender your mind, will, and emotions to the LORD and be filled with the fruit of HOLY SPIRIT.

You can also see through the Word of GOD, that demons can attack your body as well as your soul. Satan is out to steal, kill, and destroy. He is out to steal and destroy your health. In Luke 5 JESUS entered Simon Peter's house to minister to his mother-in-law who was sick with a high fever.

> *So He stood over her and rebuked the fever, and it left her.*
> *- Luke 4:39*

JESUS did not lay hands on her and declare healing. He rebuked the demon which was causing the fever to come out and the fever left her. There are demons assigned to bring affliction to our bodies. If you are one who is battling with an illness and have been praying for healing, your healing might need to come through rebuking a spirit of infirmity out of your life. I am a living testimony to this truth.

For years I had been under the care of a neurologist with a diagnosis of multiple sclerosis. I was in my 20's when the symptoms first occurred. I was in and out of the hospital every couple of months because of relapses. I had difficulty walking, my speech was slurred as if I had a stroke and I had difficulty swallowing. Because of the severity of the disease, I had to quit work and apply for social security disability. Physically I was not able to continue working, but mentally I was not prepared to stop. I loved my job and I loved serving the LORD, but the illness caused such fatigue, I had to quit my job and my work for the LORD was very limited. I was on social security disability for over ten years until the LORD intervened in my life.

One day I met with my pastors to talk about a couple of visions I had. As I was sharing, I began to feel this huge lump in my throat, as if something wanted to choke me. It was a demonic manifestation and my pastors started ministering to me. They prayed for me and began rebuking the demon that was tormenting me. They ordered the spirit of infirmity to come out. I let out a huge scream. It felt like something had left my body. They anointed me with oil and prayed for healing over my nervous system. Something happened and I knew the LORD set me free and healed me from multiple sclerosis.

That night my husband and I were sleeping. At 3:00 in the morning, our CD player began playing. Neither one of us had set the timer on the player. The song that was playing was, "Come, oh come and fill this temple with the glory of the LORD." I told my husband that GOD was confirming my healing. The next morning, I woke up and put myself through a few tests the neurologist puts me through. There were things I could do that I was not able to do in over twelve years such as walking a straight line, finger-to-nose coordination exercise, and walking on my tiptoes and heels of my feet.

The following month I kept my doctor's appointment so I could receive the medical confirmation. As I spoke with the neurologist, I asked him if he believed in divine healing and shared with him that GOD had healed me. He listened to what I had to say and said he wanted to examine me. After examining me he stated, "Pam I have been doctoring you for nine years now. I have seen you at your best and I have seen you at your worst and you have never had a perfect exam. Today you have a perfectly normal exam and I receive what you are telling me. He dismissed me as a patient and said in the future if I need to see him, give him a call. That was in 1999. I give YESHUA all the praise and glory for my divine healing.

Not all sickness is healed in this way. Many scriptures support the relationship between sin and sickness. Previously I mentioned how JESUS forgave and healed the paralytic. Apostle Paul addresses the sin of sexual immorality amongst Christians in the book of Corinthians.

> *It is actually reported that there is sexual immorality among you, and such sexual immorality as is not even named among the Gentiles – that a man has his father's wife! And you are puffed up and have not rather mourned, that he who has done this deed might be taken away from among you. For I indeed, as absent in body but present in spirit, have already judged (as though I were present) him who has so done this deed. In the name of our Lord Jesus Christ, when you are gathered together, along with my spirit, with the power of our Lord Jesus Christ, deliver such a one to Satan for the destruction of the flesh that his spirit may be saved in the day of the Lord Jesus.*
>
> *- 1 Corinthians 5:1-5*

In the above passage, the legal right and open door to bodily torment is sin. Those trapped in the sin of sexual immorality have opened the door for Satan to bring accusation and attack their flesh through sexually transmitted infections such as gonorrhea, herpes, or AIDS.

I remember Ester, a sister in the LORD who is also used in the deliverance ministry, sharing an experience she had while ministering to a lady who had a brain tumor. "Sarah was a

Christian and her neighbor practiced witchcraft. She did not trust her neighbor and felt this lady was placing curses over her. One day she found a doll with pins in its head at her doorstep. Over the next several weeks she began to experience headaches. The headaches continued for several months and grew in severity. She went to the doctor and through x-rays, a brain tumor was discovered. She did not want to undergo surgery and asked Ester to pray for her. As Sarah shared her story HOLY SPIRIT revealed to Ester the woman had resentment towards the neighbor who was a witch. Her resentment was an open door to allow the curse of witchcraft to come upon her. When Ester confronted Sarah with the resentment, she confessed her sin and asked the LORD for forgiveness."

Through her confession and renouncing to the resentment the LORD used Esther to break the curse of witchcraft off Sarah. For several days Sarah did not have any headaches. She went back to the doctors and asked to have the x-rays repeated. To the doctor's surprise, the tumor was gone. The LORD performed a miracle in the life of Sarah, but it wasn't until she confessed the resentment she had. May GOD receive all the glory for Sarah's deliverance and healing!

As stated at the beginning of this chapter, some believe that once you become a Christian your past is forgiven, and you are automatically set free from any demonic entities from the past. Through the following example from the book of Acts, this belief is refuted. In Acts 8:9-24 we read where Simon the sorcerer came to salvation after hearing the preaching of Philip. Before his salvation, he practiced witchcraft and many in Samaria recognized his great power. Verse 13 tells us Simon believed and was baptized in the faith.

> *Then Simon himself also believed; and when he was baptized, he continued with Philip, and was amazed, seeing the miracles and signs which were done.*
>
> *- Acts 8:13*

Why Do I Struggle?

As you continue reading in the passage, Peter and John came from Jerusalem to pray for the believers of Samaria to receive the baptism of HOLY SPIRIT. As the apostles lay hands on the believers, the power of HOLY SPIRIT came upon them. Simon saw this manifestation and offered the apostles money so he too could receive this power. If you recall, before salvation, Simon was a sorcerer. People paid him to perform witchcraft on them. There was a part of his past that he needed to be set free from. Simon thought he could buy the power of HOLY SPIRIT, just as in the past when people paid him, and the demonic powers of sorcery manifested. Peter rebuked him and told Simon his heart was full of bitterness and bound by iniquity. This is a believer who was baptized in the faith. There was still a part of his past, through open doors of witchcraft that needed to be closed. When Peter confronted his sin, Simon asked Peter to pray that none of the things which he spoke would come upon him.

The works of the enemy are real, and demons exist. My personal experience with demonic strongholds and the LORD setting me free has put a passion in my heart to see others tormented by the grips of the enemy set free. If you open your heart to receive help, you too can be set free. There is a tremendous battle going on in the spiritual realm for your soul. You cannot discredit the reality of Satan and the influence he can have on your life. I do not believe as a Christian you can be demon-possessed. However, a demon can exist in your body and soul through demonic influences and strongholds. If your thoughts, emotions, and actions are not controlled by HOLY SPIRIT, they are under demonic control and you need deliverance. Don't live in bondage. Allow HOLY SPIRIT to take control of your life and find your freedom through the precious blood of JESUS.

Questions for Thought
1. According to 1 Thessalonians 5:23, what are three aspects of an individual's life that must be completely sanctified?
2. As a believer, which of these areas can Satan attack?
3. What is the difference between demonic possession and demonic influence?
4. What protects you from becoming demon-possessed?

Chapter 4
HOW CAN I OBTAIN MY FREEDOM?

D o you feel bound by sin and wish you could find a way to get set free? I want you to know that if you have a personal relationship with JESUS, through Him you have the power to overcome the darkness in your life.

Deliverance is not something mystical, nor do you have to be a mature Christian to understand the process. The more proactive you become in your deliverance, the quicker your freedom will be. I have found the more desperate an individual is to hate sin and wanting a drastic change in his/her life, the easier it is for the person to be set free.

Six steps are vital and need to be followed if you want to receive deliverance and complete freedom. They include the following: Recognize, repent, renounce, rebuke, remove, and restore. The first step in a deliverance process is to recognize you are a sinner and that you need JESUS, the Messiah as your Savior. It is time to stop making excuses for your behavior or blaming others for the way you act. Own up to your actions and call them for what they are, SIN. It is only through the blood of JESUS that we can find forgiveness and freedom from sin. You must recognize the sins you have allowed to come into your life, whether knowingly or unknowingly. If you hide sin and are not open and honest with yourself or with the individuals who are helping with your deliverance process, your freedom will not come. It is very important to ask HOLY SPIRIT to reveal any hidden sin in your heart. David had a heart for GOD and wanted to please Him. That is why he asked GOD to show him if there was any wickedness in him.

Search me, O God, and know my heart; try me, and know my anxieties, and see if there is any wicked way in me.
- *Psalms 139:23*

When you ask GOD to show you what is truly in your heart, be willing to hear and see what the LORD wants to reveal to you. He will use others to point out your sins. Many times, you ask Him to show you, but when He does, you deny them, or you have difficulty accepting responsibility for the things He reveals. This is part of our sinful nature. Adam blamed Eve, and Eve blamed the serpent (Genesis 3:12-13). Who are you blaming for your actions? Recognizing and taking responsibility go hand in hand.

Once you recognize you are a sinner, you then must repent of your sins. Deliverance is based on repentance. Merriam-Webster's Dictionary defines repent as the act of feeling regret; to turn from sin and dedicate oneself to the amendment of one's life.[1]

He who covers his sins will not prosper, but whoever confesses and forsakes them will have mercy.
- *Proverbs 28:13*

Have you taken responsibility for your actions?

It is not enough to just confess your sins. You need to take responsibility for your actions and be willing to make changes in your life and turn away from your old sinful ways. Those changes can only come if you allow HOLY SPIRIT to bring the transformation which you so desperately need.

If you have never accepted JESUS as your LORD and Savior, there is no better time than now. This is needed before your deliverance process. It will change your life forever. Here is a simple prayer to begin your relationship with the LORD.

Heavenly FATHER,

I recognize that I am a sinner and I ask forgiveness for my sins. I want to turn my life around. Thank you for sending your Son who died on the cross for my sins. JESUS, cleanse me of all my sins and become LORD of my life. Deliver me from every stronghold in my life that hinders me from following Your commandments. I ask You HOLY SPIRIT to guide me in all paths of truth and help me to follow GOD's plan for my life. In JESUS's name, I pray. Amen!

How can I stop Satan's legal right?

The third step in the deliverance process is to renounce. According to the Merriam-Webster Dictionary, renounce means to give up or to refuse to follow or obey[2]. When you renounce a spirit, you are refusing to allow that spirit to dominate you. You are telling Satan he no longer has a legal right to control that area of our life. For example: If you renounce a spirit of anger, you are telling Satan you are no longer going to allow anger to dictate your life.

Areas to consider when renouncing are demonic strongholds, generational spirits, curses, soul ties, and any vows that you may have made. Generational spirits are spirits that plague your family line. Maybe your father and or grandfather fell into adultery, and you are struggling with sexual immorality. Even if you do not have any area of sexual immorality, renounce that generational spirit so it doesn't come upon you in the future.

Words can bring blessings to our lives, but they can also bring curses. "You're so stupid", "I'm so fat", "I wish I were dead", "You're never going to amount to anything" are examples of curses we place upon ourselves or on other individuals. Renounce them and break them off your life.

Soul ties can come when two individuals vow to be together for the rest of their lives. Sexual intimacy will also create a soul tie. The relationship doesn't last, but you emotionally have difficulty letting go. It is because there is a soul tie that hasn't been broken. Also, if you have any pictures or gift items from your former relationship, don't keep them. They can be a reminder of your past and keep you in bondage. You may need to renounce your favorite song you listened to together. The enemy will use all these things to try to keep you bound. Renounce any soul tie you may have from former relationships.

If you have ever spoken words such as "I will never forgive so and so" or "I swear I will never forgive you", these are vows of unforgiveness and must be renounced and canceled. I learned the importance of this while ministering deliverance to a lady. She was struggling with not being able to forgive her husband. He asked forgiveness for something he had done wrong and she could tell he truly meant it. She was able to forgive him when he asked for forgiveness, but weeks later the unforgiveness came back. She would get upset with him over simple things. She had renounced the unforgiveness and the spirit was rebuked from her, but that spirit would continue to surface. HOLY SPIRIT revealed she had made a vow of unforgiveness and it needed to be broken. Once she canceled the words "I will never forgive him", the vow was broken. She is now able to forgive her husband when he makes a mistake and the unforgiveness does not return. See the importance of asking HOLY SPIRIT to guide and show you any open doors as you go through the process of renouncing?

How do demons leave?

The next step in the deliverance process is to rebuke the spirits out of an individual. Command the demons to leave in the name of JESUS. The demons, when given the command, must leave. If they do not it is because of unconfessed sin, an unknown sin, or the individual is not desperate enough to want to be free. Deliverance must be a desire in the heart of the individual. JESUS gave His disciples both authority and power over all demons.

Then He called His twelve disciples together and gave them
power and authority over all demons, and to cure diseases.
- Luke 9:1

"And these signs will follow those who believe: In My name, they will cast out demons."

- Mark 16:17

Recognize that you have the same authority. You are given that same authority and power because of your spiritual heritage in JESUS, your Messiah. In faith utilize it! It is a shame that most churches do not teach this spiritual truth, nor do they believe deliverance is necessary. That is why many believers are bound, oppressed, and lacking the joy of the LORD in their lives.

An important step in the process of deliverance is to do a spring cleaning and remove things from your home that may be open doors for the enemy to bring accusations and keep you bound. I will talk more about this in future chapters. Ask HOLY SPIRIT to show you what needs to go.

How can I put a seal on my deliverance?

Begin praying and declaring the opposite the enemy had you bound in. If you rebuke the anger, ask the LORD to fill you with the spirit of peace. If you rebuke unforgiveness, ask to fill you with unconditional love.

The last step in your deliverance is restoring the heart of the LORD and possibly restoring individuals you have offended. This step may take time. Seek the LORD in how He wants to be restored. Examples of restoration I have witnessed are the following: One individual paid for his girlfriend to have an abortion. His restoration was giving an offering to *The Call* ministry of Lou Engle. This pro-life ministry was known for having rallies and prayer summits to overturn Roe v. Wade Supreme Court ruling. Another individual was asked to feed five homeless people. Yet another was asked to go to her father and ask forgiveness for not respecting him in her teenage years.

These are the basic steps of deliverance: recognize, repent, renounce, rebuke, remove, and restore. Remember, deliverance is a process. Once you are set free it is important to fill your life with the things of GOD. Pray, read the Word of GOD, listen to Christian music, and seek to live a Christ-centered life. If not, the demons will try to come back, and you will end up worse off than before you began the deliverance process.

> "When an unclean spirit goes out of a man, he goes through dry places, seeking rest, and finds none. Then he says, 'I will return to my house from which I came.' And when he comes, he finds it empty, swept, and put in order. Then he goes and takes with him seven other spirits more wicked than himself, and they enter and dwell there, and the last state of that man is worse than the first. So shall it also be with this wicked generation."
>
> - Matthew 12:43-45

Deliverance must be taken seriously. Before beginning your process, it is important to fast, pray, and seek HOLY SPIRIT so He can reveal to you any open doors that have allowed curses to come upon your life. Ask HOLY SPIRIT to reveal any generational sins that give the enemy a right to torment you. GOD wants to see His people free, so when you seek HOLY SPIRIT, He will lead you to all truth. Allow HOLY SPIRIT to be your guide as you seek your freedom.

Questions for Thought
1. Why is recognizing your sin an important first step in deliverance?
2. What is repentance?
3. What does the word renounce mean?
4. When we renounce, what are we telling Satan?
5. What does it mean to rebuke a demon?

SECTION 2

A CLOSER LOOK AT
GOD'S COMMANDMENTS

Chapter 5

LAW OR NO LAW?

There is a huge misconception that when JESUS came, He abolished the Law and the Old Testament is no longer significant. This is far from the truth. JESUS said:

> *"Do not think that I came to destroy the Law or the Prophets. I did not come to destroy but to fulfill. For assuredly, I say to you, till heaven and earth pass away, one jot or one tittle will by no means pass from the law till all is fulfilled."*
> *- Matthew 5:17-18*

The purpose of the Law and the Prophets was to teach people to love GOD, to worship Him, and obey His commandments. GOD used His prophets throughout scripture to point out the sins of a rebellious people and call them to repentance. Every prophecy concerning the birth, death, and resurrection of JESUS has come to pass. JESUS did not come to do away with the Law. Rather He respected it, loved it, lived it, and He fulfilled it. In verse 17, the word fulfill in the original Greek is *pleroo* which means to fill up, to fulfill, to complete, to accomplish[1].

Throughout His ministry, JESUS taught repentance. JESUS came to make complete the laws of GOD and fulfill the spiritual intent of the Law. What do I mean by this? JESUS revealed the spiritual meaning and intent of the Law, not just the letter of the Law. He taught His disciples the spiritual meaning and the application of

33

each of GOD's commandments. For example, JESUS said this about the seventh commandment:

> *"You have heard that it was said to those of old, 'You shall not commit adultery.' But I say to you that whoever looks at a woman to lust for her has already committed adultery with her in his heart."*
>
> *- Matthew 5:27-28*

What is the Spirit of the Law?

Do not commit adultery was the letter of the Law, one can understand its words clearly. However, JESUS makes the commandment far more binding and complete in the spiritual realm. It has a much deeper implication. Even though you do not commit adultery, that does not justify your lustful thoughts. Each of us will be held accountable for any adulterous thoughts, even if no physical act is committed. This is what is meant by the Spirit of the Law. The LORD is not just looking at our actions, He is searching for the attitude of our heart.

JESUS also fulfilled the Law through His death on the cross for our sins. JESUS brought to completion of the physical rituals of the Law. The animal sacrifices offered for sin were no longer needed. JESUS, the Lamb of GOD, became the ultimate sacrifice for our sins. All we need to do is to repent and ask Him into our hearts.

If you reference back to Chapter 5 of the book of Matthew, JESUS said the following:

> *"For assuredly, I say to you, till heaven and earth pass away, one jot or one title will by no means pass from the law till all is fulfilled."*
>
> *– Matthew 5:18*

The original Greek word for fulfilled in this verse is *ginomai* which means cause to be, to become with great intense[2]. JESUS is saying the Ten Commandments are here to stay and cannot be altered until all is fulfilled. When will that be? When JESUS comes back for His bride, the Church. When He returns, you will no longer need them because you will be in His presence for eternity. But until then, align yourselves with the design GOD established and embrace His instructions so you can live a victorious life.

Questions for Thought

1. What did JESUS mean when He said He came to fulfill the Law and the Prophets?
2. What is the difference between the letter of the Law and the Spirit of the Law?

Chapter 6
RELIGION OR RELATIONSHIP?

G OD introduces the Ten Commandments by stating the following:

> *"I am the LORD your God who brought you out of the land of Egypt, out of the house of bondage."*
>
> *- Exodus 20:2*

GOD is making a declaration of who He is, He is a personal GOD! That is why He said, "I am the LORD **your** GOD." How do you see GOD? Do you see Him very distant and unreachable, this superpower somewhere in heaven? You are not alone. Many people have been Christian for years yet have never felt close to GOD. Although this may be the norm for most people, this is not the way GOD intended your relationship to be with Him.

Your walk with GOD is not about having a religion, it's about having a relationship. He wants you to enjoy a personal relationship with Him. Religious activities apart from fellowship with GOD are meaningless rituals. GOD wants to manifest His presence in your life. He wants you to feel His presence while you pray, as you worship Him, and as you converse with Him throughout your day. He wants you to have a personal encounter and develop a close fellowship with Him. Many individuals love the LORD and want a deeper relationship with Him but don't know how to pursue it. You may be one of them. I think we make things too complicated. Throughout scripture,

GOD desires to love and be loved. It's that simple. He wants to be LORD of your life and for you to follow in His ways.

Is GOD reachable?

GOD does not want you to know Him from a distance as some unreachable God up in heaven, He wants you to know Him in a personal and intimate way. He doesn't want you to just pray to Him, He wants you to have a conversation with Him. Fellowship with GOD is having a two-way conversation with Him. You share with Him what is on your heart and listen to hear what is on His heart. If you read in the Book of Exodus you will recall how Moses encouraged the Israelites not to fear GOD and to draw close to Him. The Israelites were too afraid to hear from GOD themselves. They wanted to hear from GOD through Moses rather than having a personal encounter.

> *Now all the people witnessed the thunderings, the lightning flashes, the sound of the trumpet, and the mountain smoking; and when the people saw it, they trembled and stood afar off. Then they said to Moses, "You speak with us, and we will hear; but let not God speak with us, lest we die." And Moses said to the people, "Do no fear; for God has come to test you, and that His fear may be before you, so that you may not sin." So the people stood afar off, but Moses drew near the thick darkness where God was.*
> *- Exodus 20:18-21*

The people stood afar off, but Moses drew near to GOD. And what were the results? While Moses was having an encounter with GOD on the mountain top, the Israelites fell back into idolatry and their sinful ways. If your relationship with GOD is through the words of your pastor, your home church leader, your parents, or through conferences, you are missing out on a beautiful relationship with GOD. Your growth in the LORD should not depend on others. It is your responsibility to develop a personal relationship with the LORD and to seek His presence.

Your spiritual leaders are there to guide you, encourage you, correct you, and pray for you.

When you accept JESUS as your LORD and Savior you enter a covenant relationship with GOD. As a believer, you are a part of His church. Many scriptures in the Bible refer to His church as the bride and JESUS as the bridegroom. Build on that love relationship. You may ask, "But how do I that?" Reflect upon a time when you were starting a new relationship? It may be with a girlfriend, a boyfriend, or someone you just met. Do you remember how awkward you felt at first because you didn't know what to say or what to do? You probably began the relationship by asking a bunch of questions about each other so you could learn about the other individual.

The only way to get to know someone is to spend time with that person, find out their likes and dislikes, and as you do you begin to build a personal relationship with that individual. To help nurture the relationship you do things together that the other individual enjoys and avoid doing or saying things that might offend the person. It's no different when you develop a relationship with GOD. Talk to Him, let Him know what is on your mind. Ask GOD what is on His heart. Find out His likes and dislikes through reading His Word. GOD is calling each of us to have an intimate relationship with Him. It is not about having a head knowledge of JESUS. It is a love relationship that builds through intimately knowing Him.

How can I draw close to GOD?

One of the key components in developing a relationship with GOD is to develop a relationship with HOLY SPIRIT. HOLY SPIRIT is not a thing, HOLY SPIRIT is the third person of a triune GOD. JESUS prayed to the FATHER, and GOD gave us HOLY SPIRIT.

> *"If you love Me, keep My commandments. And I will pray the Father, and He will give you another Helper, that He may abide with you forever....But the Helper, the Holy Spirit, whom the Father will send in My name, He will teach*

38

you all things, and bring to your remembrance all things that I said to you."

- John 14:15-16, 26

When you receive JESUS as your Savior, HOLY SPIRIT abides inside of you. It is so important to build your relationship with HOLY SPIRIT. It is HOLY SPIRIT who brings conviction of sin and the power to overcome its grip over your life. It is HOLY SPIRIT who gives you the revelation of the Word of GOD. It is HOLY SPIRIT who will guide you in all truth. As you fellowship with HOLY SPIRIT you will come to know and comprehend the thoughts of GOD.

For what man knows the things of a man except the spirit of the man which is in him? Even so, no one knows the things of God except the Spirit of God. Now we have received, not the spirit of the world, but the Spirit who is from God, that we might know the things that have been freely given to us by God.

- 1 Corinthians 2:11-12

Do you want to draw close to GOD? Look for Him with all your heart. Draw close to HOLY SPIRIT, He is the only one who can reveal the truths of GOD to you. Learn to hear His voice. Listen for the still, small voice speaking to your heart. Many times, HOLY SPIRIT is speaking to you, you just don't recognize His voice. As you wait quietly for GOD's presence or as you meditate on the Word, invite HOLY SPIRIT to come and abide with you. Ask Him to speak to you. There is so much HOLY SPIRIT wants to release into your life. Learn to discern His still, small voice speaking to your heart. Don't listen to the lies of the enemy, thinking this could never happen to you. Keep seeking intimacy with HOLY SPIRIT. That is what Marsha did and her knowledge of GOD changed from a religious mindset to a beautiful relationship with GOD.

"I learned about Christianity in a Methodist church. They taught me to recite prayers and sing hymns. I became an expert in the "potluck dinner" and running a soup kitchen. My days were filled with planned events and community outreaches, camping trips, and Bible studies. However, no matter how full my days were and how many prayers and hymns I could recite from memory, it always seemed like something was missing. My life had an emptiness that I could not explain. Because of a hunger for more things of the LORD, I began to search for other churches to see what they had to offer. As I visited other churches, I realized my relationship with GOD was superficial. Then something started to happen. I started to fall in love with the things of GOD. The Word of GOD came to life and started to transform my understanding of what it meant to be a Christian. My relationship changed from a head knowledge into a beautiful personal relationship with JESUS, my LORD, and Savior whom I now hold dear to my heart.

I discovered that GOD was very much alive and wants more than just cold routines from me. He wanted me. He wanted to talk with me and know everything about me. GOD wanted to know my fears and dreams and be with me in every moment- good, bad, and ugly. He wanted a real, live relationship with me. It was like my eyes started to open to who JESUS was and what it meant to be a Christian. This intimacy began the process of deliverance in my life.

I still remember the first time I learned that I could talk to HOLY SPIRIT. He is as much GOD as the Father and the Son. Our relationship with GOD is through a relationship with HOLY SPIRIT. I was in a meeting and someone addressed their prayer directly to HOLY SPIRIT. I think my jaw dropped. I thought to myself, "But you can't do that" and "is that even allowed?" After the meeting, I questioned the individual. She taught me that HOLY SPIRIT is our counselor and friend and wants to hear from us. I still have not recovered from that moment. My GOD, the GOD of

Abraham, Isaac, and Jacob, wants to know me and have a personal relationship with me. What a life-changing experience and revelation this was for my life, and I have not been the same since."

Marsha's victory came when she realized GOD didn't want her religion, He wanted a personal relationship with her. Through her process, she came to realize her emptiness was due to the lack of intimacy with HOLY SPIRIT. Her emptiness is now filled with the friendship and fellowship of HOLY SPIRIT. You, too, can embrace His friendship and fellowship if you keep seeking. GOD is yearning to have an encounter with you. The Word of GOD promises that those who seek Him will find Him. Don't give up, press in until you have the breakthrough you are looking for. Grab hold of this promise and don't let go of it until you receive it.

> *"Ask, and it will be given to you; seek, and you will find; knock, and it will be opened to you. For everyone who asks receives, and he who seeks finds, and to him who knocks it will be opened. Or what man is there among you who, if his son asks for bread, will give him a stone? Or if he asks for a fish, will he give him a serpent? If you then, being evil, know how to give good gifts to your children, how much more will your Father who is in heaven give good things to those who ask Him."*
>
> *- Matthew 7:7-11*

> *"As the Father loved Me, I also have loved you; abide in My love."*
>
> *- John 15:9*

Do you truly love GOD?

Don't settle for a head knowledge of this love. JESUS is inviting you to dwell in His love. He gave His life so you can be set free from the bondage of sin, the eternal judgment of hell, and enjoy the blessings He has for your life when you accept Him as your LORD and Savior. GOD fulfilled His part of the love covenant by giving us salvation through JESUS, the Messiah. Webster's dictionary defines covenant as a formal and serious agreement or promise between two or more individuals.[1] When you pray and ask JESUS into your life, it is not just a simple prayer that you take lightly. It is a promise of a commitment you are making with GOD. You are entering into a love covenant. Fulfill your part of the covenant.

> *"For this is the covenant that I will make with the house of Israel after those days, says the LORD: I will put My laws in their mind and write them on their hearts, and I will be their God, and they shall be My people."*
>
> *- Hebrews 8:10*

If you truly love GOD, His commandments will be in your mind and on your heart. You will make a conscious effort to do everything you can to walk in obedience according to His Word. You are doing this because of your love for GOD and not because of an unhealthy fear of punishment. A genuine love for GOD produces wholehearted obedience. Obedience without love is legalism. Your relationship with GOD should not be based on a set of dos and don'ts. That is seeing Him through a religious mindset. See it as GOD's way of protecting you. He is shielding you from the schemes of your enemy, Satan, who is out to kill, steal, and destroy your life. When you walk in obedience, you are demonstrating to GOD your love towards Him. Don't fear Him for what He will do to you because of your sin. Have a holy reverence fear of GOD, one that causes you to run from sin because of your love for Him.

My life is so messed up! Can GOD fix it?

Sin separates you from GOD. Most often, that is why you feel so distant from Him. Are you struggling with sin and allowing that to keep you distant from GOD? Do you feel guilty for turning your back on Him and feel you are not worthy to have a relationship with Him? Guilt is not from GOD. However, the conviction of sin is. Remember the parable of the lost sheep and how the owner of the sheep left the ninety-nine and went looking for the one that was lost.

"And when he comes home, he calls together his friends and neighbors, saying to them, 'Rejoice with me, for I have found my sheep which was lost!' I say to you that likewise there will be more joy in heaven over one sinner who repents than over ninety-nine just persons who need no repentance."
- Luke 15:6-7

It doesn't matter how tangled up your life is right now. GOD can untangle it and transform your life. Angels will rejoice in heaven when you come back to your relationship with Heavenly FATHER. Don't ever think your life is so bad that GOD will never forgive you. That is a lie from the enemy. There is hope for your situation and that hope is in JESUS. GOD loves you so much, He provided an avenue of escape for your sins. JESUS is the bridge between you and GOD. He died on the cross for your sins, so you can have eternal life. You can draw closer to GOD and close that gap by asking forgiveness, repenting of your sins, and receiving JESUS as your personal Savior. If you once served GOD but have turned your back on Him, rededicate your life to Him. What are you waiting for? He's waiting for you. Don't postpone it another minute. The LORD has beautiful things in store for your life. If you want a closer relationship with the LORD here is a simple prayer for you:

Heavenly FATHER,
I want to draw closer to you. I don't want religion. I want a personal relationship with You. I ask forgiveness for seeing you through the eyes of religion. I ask forgiveness for doing things with a religious mindset and following man-made formulas rather than being led by HOLY SPIRIT. I renounce the spirit of religion and the spirit of legalism. I rebuke the spirit of religion and legalism out of my life. I ask You HOLY SPIRIT to invade my

life and bring the transformation that I need so that I can have a deep encounter with You. I receive the intimate relationship You have for me. Teach me how to walk daily in our love relationship. In JESUS's name, I pray. Amen!

Questions for Thought

1. What does Exodus 20:2 tell us about our relationship with GOD?
2. What is the wrong perspective of fearing GOD?
3. What is the proper perspective of fearing GOD?
4. How can you show your love to GOD?

Chapter 7

THE WEIGHT IS OFF, NOW WHAT?

*"I am the LORD your God who brought you out of the land of
Egypt, out of the house of bondage."*
- Exodus 20:2

A s you continue to focus on this scripture that introduces the
Ten Commandments, you will understand the purpose of
your ultimate freedom. The second component of this scripture
is about being set free from your bondage of sin and GOD's
purpose for doing so. At first glance of this scripture, you may
believe GOD is talking to the people of Israel and how He rescued
them from the hands of Pharaoh. You may be thinking, "This
doesn't have anything to do with me. I wasn't a slave in Egypt."
However, if you go back to the Hebrew root of this passage, the
word for Egypt is *Mitsrayim*[1]. It stems from a Hebraic root which
means to bind (shackle or imprison). It is synonymous with
bondage. What is your bondage? It is sin! GOD wants to
personally set you free from your bondage of sin.

> *Jesus answered them, "Most assuredly, I say to you,
> 'whoever commits sin is a slave of sin."*
> *- John 8:34*

Your Egypt is the sin that keeps you bound. Receiving JESUS as
your personal Savior is the easy part, leaving your sins behind
and not turning back to your sinful ways is the challenge. It is

45

only through the precious blood of JESUS, who can deliver you from the bondage of sin. He alone is the only one who can set you free from the grips of evil. It is the power of HOLY SPIRIT that gives you the strength to overcome any temptation that comes your way.

One day I was preparing a message to preach on a Sunday night. My pastor was out of town and he asked me to bring a message for the church. While preparing the message, I began asking GOD questions. "Why did the Israelites fall back into their old ways just three days after You parted the Red Sea and freed them from the hands of Pharaoh?" Why is it even though GOD moves in our lives, we fall back into the snare of sin? The LORD answered my questions and I used the following illustration in the impartation in hopes that HOLY SPIRIT would bring the conviction.

One individual in the congregation hated mushrooms. In preparation for the preaching, I cooked a dish with mushrooms and chicken to use as an illustration. At one point in the message, I asked Emily to come up and I offered her the dish of mushrooms. I even told her they were organic and had some seasonings on them that she liked. I asked her to try them. Emily said, "No, I can't". I even had a piece of organic chicken to go with them. Surely as she ate the chicken, it would help to hide the taste of the mushrooms. She still refused. I then waved a $50 bill in front of her and told her if she ate the mushrooms, I would give her $50. Emily refused again and I asked her, "Why can't I bribe you into eating these mushrooms?" She replied, "Because I hate them, and they will make me sick."

Why is it when Satan cooks something up for your life, gives it some flavor, and makes it appealing to the taste buds that you fall into the temptation? It is because you haven't gotten to the point of hating it. You need to get to the point where Emily got with hating mushrooms. Get to the place in your life where you hate sin so much, you won't even take a nibble from it. If you are interested in hearing the message with the mushroom illustration, it can be heard by going to ABBA Ministries YouTube channel and search for "Gratitude with an Attitude" video.

If you are struggling with sin, know that there is no sin too strong that the power of the blood of JESUS can't overcome. Trust in Him to bring you your deliverance. Ask HOLY SPIRIT to give you a hatred for the sin you struggle with. I know of an individual who cried out to the LORD to deliver him from cigarettes. From that day, every time he had an urge for a cigarette and smoked it, it made him sick. Two days later he never tried a cigarette again.

Why does GOD set you free?

GOD does not set you free just so you can have your freedom. It is much deeper than just removing the weight of sin from your life. He has a purpose and plan for your life. GOD spoke to Pharaoh through Moses to let His people go. Why did GOD deliver His people out of Egypt? It was so they could worship Him.

> "And you shall say to him, the LORD God of the Hebrews has sent me to you, saying, Let My people go that they may serve Me in the wilderness."
> - Exodus 7:16

The Hebrew word for serve is *abad*, which means to work, to serve, to be a worshipper.[2] GOD takes you out of the bondage of sin so you can work to further His kingdom, serve Him, and worship Him and Him alone. Throughout my years of ministering deliverance, I have seen individuals in situations that seemed impossible to be liberated from. Most of the time your dilemmas are because of your doings. You have allowed the things of the world to overcome you and you heed to the desires of the flesh. For many, it isn't until you hit rock bottom that you search for GOD. What is the motive for you seeking your deliverance? Is it to draw closer to GOD and to serve Him? I have ministered to individuals who have made promises to the LORD that if He sets them free from their predicament, they will make things right in their life and serve Him. The LORD, in His mercies, will give you an escape to test your heart. Many individuals came for a quick fix and in time returned to their former ways. Their lives ended up worse off than before they came for deliverance.

On the other hand, I have seen individuals truly repent, get set free, and develop a beautiful relationship with the LORD. Here is a testimony of Jennifer.

"There was a time in my life when I was going to church but living a double life. I would go to the clubs on Saturday and go to church on Sunday with a hangover. This was my way of worshipping GOD. At that time, I had a job where I was making decent money, but I was not spending it wisely. Nor was I honoring GOD with my money. I was full of vanity and all I wanted was nice clothes, jewelry and hang out with my friends. I was already a single parent and was neglecting my children. I would leave them with anyone who would take them so I could party with my friends. GOD in His mercy exposed my sin and I started losing everything that took my attention away from Him. I lost my job, my car got repossessed, and the place where I was living was no longer available for rent. I was eligible for unemployment but did not receive enough income to rent another place. Therefore, each rental application was denied. A male friend tried to help me rent a place, but that door was shut also.

Seeing I was in such a predicament, my pastor suggested I go to the Orlando Union Rescue Mission which is a faith-based organization that provides shelter to families in need. I thought to myself "The last thing I will ever do is go to a shelter." Of course, I didn't say this to him, but I wrote down the information and jokingly told him I would call. As a final attempt, I decided to move in with my brother-in-law and his family temporarily until I could find a job and be able to live on my own again. I was determined to resolve my problems my way. I was there for two days when my brother-in-law received a phone call from his native country about his grandmother's death. He went to the

Dominican Republic for the funeral and I stayed with his wife and children. He called two days later to inform his wife that he decided to move back to the Dominican Republic and that he was going to send for her and the children. At this point, I realized that GOD was closing all the doors and I had no other choice than to go to the shelter. The LORD knew what it would take to break my pride. I held the paper with the information about the shelter in my hand and I said, "LORD if it is your will for me to go to this place, open the door."

I went to the shelter and had an interview. The lady told me that they usually have a waiting list, but the individuals on the waiting list have already found a place to live. One of the ladies staying at the shelter was moving out the same day and that I could move in the next day. The interviewer said this was very unusual. I knew GOD had intervened and it was His will for me to be there. He knows what it will take to set us free. GOD had to take everything away from me to get my attention. While in the shelter, the LORD broke my pride and I learned about humility. I also learned how to honor my authorities, about submission, and about serving others. I was set free in many areas of my life through a deliverance process and none of this would have happened had the LORD not brought me to the shelter and smashed my pride.

The LORD kept me at the shelter for two years. During that time, He brought the transformation I so much needed for my life. I was able to find a job and save up $9,000. This was enough money to pay most of my debts and be able to find a place of my own. GOD restored double of everything the enemy stole from me. But it all started when I repented of my sin and decided to walk in obedience. He not only restored me financially but also restored my relationship with Him. Since my deliverance, I have not turned my back on serving the LORD. Today I have the privilege of serving Him as a Home Church leader and am giving to others what the LORD has freely given to me."

Satan wanted to destroy the life of Jennifer. He had her blinded to the fact that she had a religion and not a personal relationship with GOD and her worship to the LORD was all in vain. The beginning of her testimony is exactly what GOD meant in the following scripture:

> "These people draw near to Me with their mouth, and honor Me with their lips, but their heart is far from Me. And in vain they worship Me, teaching as doctrines the commandments of men."
>
> *- Matthew 15:8-9*

I have witnessed the power of transformation in Jennifer's life. It is truly a miracle and we give GOD all the praise and glory. Your relationship with GOD is about worshipping Him and giving Him the glory and honor, He deserves. At the beginning of her testimony, Jennifer was going to church with a hangover, thinking she was fulfilling her obligation in worshipping GOD. A Greek mentality describes a worshipper as someone who goes to church on Sunday or one who has musical talent through singing or playing an instrument. True worship is a matter of the heart expressed through a lifestyle of holiness. It is about living your life according to the Word of GOD bringing honor and glory to Him.

> "But the hour is coming, and now is, when the true worshipers will worship the Father in spirit and truth; for the Father is seeking such to worship Him. God is Spirit, and those who worship Him must worship in spirit and truth."
>
> *- John 4:23-24*

You are created to worship GOD. Worship is more than just going to church. It is a lifestyle. You don't have to play an instrument or have a beautiful voice to worship Him, all you need is a passion for His presence. So many times, we rely on the worshippers on the altar, when it is a matter of the heart. How many times have you caught yourself singing in church, but your mind was distracted by the stress of the day, the argument you had with your spouse, or things you needed to do when you got home? You go through the motions of worship, but inside there is spiritual emptiness. I am sure you can agree that this happens to you from time to time. When you worship with this kind of attitude, you are not worshipping GOD in spirit and truth.

How is your worship?

One day as I was seeking the LORD, I asked Him, " LORD, what does it mean to worship in spirit and truth"? His reply was very simple but profound. He answered, *"Worship is aligning your heart with the heart of the Father to bring glory to JESUS."* GOD is seeking those whose worship is coming from a heart that cries out to Him, a heart that wants to glorify JESUS. Your worship should draw you into the presence of GOD. That is what worship is all about. It is not about going to church on Sunday or about singing a few songs to make you feel good. It is an expression of a love relationship with GOD, day by day, and moment by moment.

Is there freedom in your worship? If not, GOD wants to set you free. Are you ready to be a true worshipper for the LORD? Renounce any garment of religion and tradition from your life. Satan knows that worship draws you closer to GOD. That is why he fights so much to stop you from worshipping. Renounce any complacency or any garment of heaviness that you may be feeling. Unless there is a passion for GOD, there is no true worship. Ask HOLY SPIRIT to anoint you with passion for the things of GOD and watch the transformation come over your life.

Are you serving?

GOD does not set you free from sin so you can do what you want. He sets you free so you can have an intimate relationship with Him and serve Him in whatever capacity He asks of you. What are you doing for the Kingdom of GOD? Are you running the race or just being a spectator? Many people are so comfortable coming to church every Sunday, sitting in a pew, and receiving the Word of GOD with no desire to serve the LORD.

Does this sound like you? Or maybe you think He could never use you. GOD does not want you to be a bench warmer, there are tasks to be done for His Kingdom. You may have a desire to serve the LORD, but your fears or insecurities are stopping you from allowing GOD to use you. Is your reason for not serving because you are a young Christian or don't know the Word of GOD well enough. You can come up with many excuses for not serving the LORD. Put your trust in GOD, not in yourself. Satan is out to rob you of a beautiful destiny in serving GOD. You may not be called to be a pastor, but there are many areas where the LORD needs your help. It's not about you, it's about HOLY SPIRIT working through you. Take that step of faith and allow HOLY SPIRIT to bring the transformation to your life so you can be used in a powerful way to further GOD's kingdom.

A Christian who is not serving the LORD will never experience the power of GOD in his life. You should never be content just being a spectator. Get involved and see the potentials GOD has for your life. As you read the testimony below, I trust it will encourage you to seek the deliverance for your life so you too can be used by GOD.

"In 1982 I began my Christian walk with GOD. I asked JESUS to come into my heart and become LORD of my life. It was my first love experience with the LORD, and I thought it would bring a dramatic change to my life. My walk with GOD began in a very traditional church. Time passed by and unfortunately, after 17 years I had not grown spiritually and was in the same place when I first gave my life to the LORD. I went to the services on Sunday and I always sat in the same place. You could say that it had my name written on it.

I felt like an invisible person to the world and thought that no one even cared about me or noticed that I existed. Inside I had feelings of hatred and resentment towards my parents because they had abandoned me when I was a baby. This left a scar in my life and I suffered from insecurities and rejection. I hated my life and wanted to die. I often isolated myself and felt like something inside me wanted to explode. On two occasions I tried to kill myself. I shared with my pastor how I was feeling, and his reply was not to pay attention to this, that when I accepted JESUS in my heart, the past is forgotten. I tried to put my feelings behind me, but time passed, and I still felt the same. I wanted to be free, but no matter how hard I tried, I could not get my emotions under control.

My husband and I moved to Florida and we received a prophetic word that GOD was going to change our lives and powerfully use us. Little did I know what GOD had in store for us! Looking back, I understand why the LORD preserved my life, He had a better plan. Satan was out to rob my destiny, but GOD intervened and did not permit it. When I received that word, it brought new hope to my life. But for that word to come to pass the LORD had to do a work in me first. Due to the abandonment of my mother and father, I felt rejected and that nobody loved me. This did not allow me to advance in my spiritual life since all this made me more sensitive to any criticism that I received, even if it was made in love. I isolated myself from people because I thought they hated me, I felt ugly, stupid, and insecure. I led a very lonely life because I kept myself in a bubble and I would not allow anyone to get close to me.

Moving to Florida was from the LORD. He knew my struggles and knew where I could receive the spiritual help I needed. The LORD led me to a church that understood the spiritual realm and that demons were real and could influence a believer's life. The pastor discerned what was happening to me and explained that spirits were tormenting me. I went through a process of deliverance and was set free from rejection, isolation, self-hatred, insecurities, and lack of forgiveness towards my mother and father. For the glory of GOD, I was set free and the LORD even brought healing and restored my relationship with my mother.

After receiving my freedom, I realized that it was not the people who rejected me, but the enemy took advantage and put thoughts of rejection in my mind to destroy me and my destiny. We know that the enemy comes to kill, steal, and destroy but the

God that I serve set me free. Through the rejection, I created a bubble around me that did not allow people to approach me. How the enemy wanted to use this to bring harm to my life!

Today, I am no longer a spectator or fan sitting in a pew, I am a team player advancing the Kingdom of God. I am no longer controlled by a spirit of rejection but am led by the power of Holy Spirit. Through Him I live a life serving the Lord, preaching the gospel to the nations as He leads. God has given me a burden to help others who are trapped in religion and tradition, bringing them out of bondage and coming to a true relationship with the Lord and Holy Spirit. I live a happy life knowing that I am the daughter of *"the Great I Am"* and have found my identity in Jesus."

Many of you see Isabella ministering in the church and don't realize the price she has paid to be anointed and used by God. She surrendered everything to the Lord, and He moved powerfully in her life. She received deliverance for one purpose and that was to be used by God for His glory. The enemy will try to do everything in his power to stop you from seeking your deliverance and serving Him. God can set you free from everything that hinders you from serving Him.

GOD can't use me, or can He?

Don't ever think that you are too old or too young to be used by the Lord or that He can't use you in a way you've never been used in the past. Here is a testimony of Bianca who at the age of 81 began receiving prophetic words for individuals.

"As the youngest of eleven children in our family I was ignored and very unhappy and insecure. As I grew up, I chose to focus on trying to find happiness and love. Unfortunately, they were not good choices. All my decisions were based on serving me, me, and me. At the age of 40, I experienced a deep sense of loneliness that caused me to turn to JESUS and accept Him as my LORD and Savior. I started attending the prayer meetings and sure enough, that is what I needed to help break my loneliness. I then received teachings on HOLY SPIRIT shortly thereafter and received the baptism of HOLY SPIRIT. My life since then has been an adventure of learning who JESUS is in me and who I am in Him so I can imitate Him and serve Him as I serve others.

Fast forward another 40 years, I heard a teaching on hearing the voice of GOD. I followed their suggestions and focused on listening for the voice of GOD. Through daily journaling He is restoring my soul, giving me words of encouragement, hope, and love that I never received growing up. Who would ever think at the age of 81 GOD would begin to use me? I wanted GOD to use me but thought I was too old. Much to my surprise, he began using me in the prophetic. The LORD began to give me prophetic words to release to others. Following the protocol of my church, I began to release what the LORD was giving me, and I could see the hand of GOD move in these individual's lives. It gives me great pleasure to bring awareness and encouragement to others as I shared what GOD put on my heart.

As part of the ministry in our home church, we began ministering in a local nursing home. I led the worship, prayed for individuals, and preached the Word of GOD. I never dreamed I would be doing this at the age of 81. However, I am reminded that Moses started his ministry when he was 80 years old and completed his assignment at the age of 120. When GOD gives you a task to do, He will give you the strength and ability to do it.

I am ever grateful to my GOD for his patience, unconditional love, and mercy towards me. I realized you are never too old to be used in a new way by the LORD. Don't ever think GOD can't use you because of your age. Take heart, it is never too late when GOD calls because His timing is perfect."

Don't let your age intimidate you from being used by GOD. There is no age limit for Him. Have a willing heart and step out in faith, trusting GOD will provide you with everything you need to serve Him.

Is there something stopping your anointing?

I want to speak to those who are already serving the LORD. Are you experiencing the anointing of GOD in your life as you serve Him? Do you sense something is stopping you from moving forward as you serve? Are you lacking the victory GOD has for your life? Without knowing it, you may have a curse over your life because of open doors from your past before you entered a relationship with JESUS.

You should be walking in the blessings of the LORD. As I stated at the introduction of this book, when you disobey GOD's commandments, you open the door for curses to come upon you. You may not even realize you are breaking one of GOD's commandments. This does not prevent you from receiving a curse. As you read the following chapters of this book, allow HOLY SPIRIT to show you if you have unknowingly broken one of His commandments and offended the heart of GOD. Close those doors, cancel the curses, and walk in the blessings GOD has for your life.

Questions for Thought
1. What is your Egypt?
2. For what purpose does GOD set you free?
3. According to Matthew 15:8-9, how can we worship GOD in vain?
4. What does it mean to be a true worshipper of GOD?

Chapter 8
WHY DO I FEEL SO OPPRESSED?

Commandment One
"You shall have no other gods before Me."
- Exodus 20:3

Have you ever felt oppression come over you and wonder why you feel the way you do? I'm not talking about feeling depressed when things happen to you such as having a loved one die. I'm talking about when things would seem fine one day, but the next day feeling an unexplainable heaviness and lack of joy. Do you try to draw close to GOD and feel like a wall or resistance is separating you from Him and not allowing you to feel the intimacy you so desire? The enemy is out to steal your joy and allow oppression to come over you so you will lose your passion to seek after GOD. It is His desire for you to have intimacy with Him. As you read through this chapter, ask HOLY SPIRIT to reveal the root of your oppression so that it can be uprooted from your life.

What is lingering from your past?

The spiritual realm is real. Your relationship with GOD is through HOLY SPIRIT. When you ask JESUS into your life, HOLY SPIRIT comes and lives inside of you. He dwells within your spirit. The more you fill yourself with HOLY SPIRIT, the more of GOD's attributes will be inside of you. GOD is a holy GOD! He is a jealous GOD and He does not want to compete with any other spirit in your life. Think of it this way. I am sure all of us have been in love with someone on at least one occasion. It may have been in your teenage years when you had a crush on someone or a lasting relationship that ended for one reason or another. For healing to take place and for you to move on in your life, remove those things that remind you of your former relationship. Removing items that were bought by or remind you of your ex is necessary. Otherwise, those things can hold you in bondage.

The same is true when you begin your relationship with GOD. When you ask JESUS into your life, GOD forgives your sins. However, before coming to the LORD there may be things that you have done that opened doors to the spiritual realm which keeps you from receiving total freedom. Satan is an accuser and he goes before GOD making accusations against you. These accusations are because of past sins or sins of your ancestors which you have not renounced. There may even be things in your possession that the enemy uses to claim legal rights to torment you. That is why deliverance is so important in the life of a believer. Ask HOLY SPIRIT to reveal any spirits that may influence your life because of your past religious beliefs, practices, or relationships.

Where do you seek direction for your life?

GOD's first commandment states that He wants no other god before Him. He wants no part of your former spiritual life, nor does He want you involved in any other spirit other than HOLY SPIRIT. There may be open doors from your past because of involvement with sorcery or witchcraft that needs to be closed. There may also be some practices that you are not aware of that open the door to the demonic.

I know of people who follow their horoscope daily seeking direction for their life. Many believe in the predictions that are given and rely on them rather than reading GOD's Word for their guidance. You may be reading horoscopes out of curiosity just to see what it says and believe there is no harm in doing so. You are opening yourself up to the demonic and sooner or later it will influence your life. Astrology is a form of fortune-telling based upon the use of stars and planets to read into a person's past, present, and future. It attempts to advise people on how to act, based on the positions of the stars.

> *"And take heed, lest you lift your eyes to heaven, and when you see the sun, the moon, and the stars, all the host of heaven, you feel driven to worship them and serve them."*
> - *Deuteronomy 4:19*

Your trust needs to be in GOD, not in astrological predictions such as horoscopes. Whether you realize it or not, you are seeking guidance from demonic sources when you turn to horoscope reading, fortune tellers, mediums, or spiritualists. GOD gives warning to such practices.

> *"Woe to the rebellious children", says the LORD, "Who take counsel, but not of Me, and who devise plans, but not of My Spirit, that they may add sin to sin".*
> - *Isaiah 30:1*

Seek direction for your life through GOD's Word and ask HOLY SPIRIT to guide you as you put your trust in Him. He will give you the direction you need for your life. When you open the door to demonic practices you are falling into a deceptive trap of the enemy. The following is a testimony of one sister in the LORD who fell into such deception.

"Before coming to the feet of JESUS I used to look for solutions to my problems in many ways, but they were corrupt ways. I was lost and ignorant because I did not know JESUS, nor did I know His Word and the promises of His Word. Because I did not know the truth I got involved in all types of witchcraft and divination. I became addicted to reading my horoscope. My whole life revolved around reading it. Every day I would read my horoscope to see what the day held for my life. My decisions for the day depended on what my horoscope predicted for my life. I had a total dependence on the horoscope, not realizing the path of darkness it was taking me down.

I hit a very low point in my life and realized I was heading down a road of destruction. GOD has a purpose and plan for my life, and I was allowing Satan to pull me away from my destiny. GOD allowed circumstances in my life to occur to get me to a point of brokenness and surrender to Him. Through my desperation, I turned my life over to JESUS and fell completely in love with him. The more I sought Him, the more my soul thirsted and hungered for his presence. Things began to change, and my circumstances improved. I had repented from my heart and asked forgiveness for my past, but still, I felt obstacles were stopping me from moving forward in my walk with the LORD. I came to realize that it was because I had opened doors to generational curses because of my involvement with the occult. Out of ignorance, I had made a covenant with darkness. I was bound with impurity, giving rights to the devil to destroy me and I knew I needed to be set free from my past.

Through prayer, the LORD led me to a church where they understood the spiritual realm and welcomed those who needed and wanted to go through a process of deliverance. I repented of my sins, renounced every open door to my past, and broke every covenant I made with the occult. Through the blood of JESUS, every yoke of darkness was broken off my life. I am no longer bound to the horoscopes that once dictated my life. My trust is in the LORD. His plans, purposes, dreams, and destiny are being fulfilled in my life. All for the Glory of His name."

Before her deliverance, Pricilla was heading down a road of destruction. The bondage of the occult was strong in her life, but as she asked forgiveness and renounced every open door of the occult, she and was able to find the freedom she was searching for. The Word of GOD tells us that we are not to practice witchcraft or magic.

> *"When you come into the land which the* Lord *your God is giving you, you shall not learn to follow the abominations of those nations. There shall not be found among you anyone who makes his son or his daughter pass through the fire, or one who practices witchcraft, or a soothsayer, or one who interprets omens, or a sorcerer, or one who conjures spells, or a medium, or a spiritist, or one who calls up the dead. For all who do these things are an abomination to the* Lord, *and because of these abominations the* Lord *your God drives them out from before you. You shall be blameless before the* Lord *your God. For these nations which you will dispossess listened to soothsayers and diviners; but as for you, the* Lord *your God has not appointed such for you."*
> *- Deuteronomy 18:9-14*

We are instructed in God's Word not to call upon the dead. This is necromancy and in doing so you are invoking familiar spirits. If you have been to a medium or sorcerer in the past, renounce that. One mistake I see many Christians doing is talking to their deceased relative. The enemy is subtle and without realizing it you can open the door to the spirit of darkness. I have read many posts on Facebook of people sharing a conversation with their deceased loved one. It is one thing to honor the memory of your family member, but to engage in a conversation with them is unbiblical.

Who do you call upon?

God wants to be Lord of your life. You have God's Word to guide you and you have Holy Spirit you can call upon. You don't need to seek answers for your life from any other spiritual sources. The Bible is very clear about this. They will defile the body, bring curses to your life, and lead you astray. Not only that, spirits of witchcraft attract other spirits of the occult. This happened in the life of Silvia. May her testimony open your eyes to the reality of the spiritual world and the stronghold it can bring upon your life.

"I grew up believing in everything of the occult: witchcraft, sorcery, superstition, and divination. My faith was placed in man where there was no biblical basis and the Word of GOD tells us - Cursed is the man who trusts in man! We would have family gatherings and two of my aunts would call upon the spirits. The spirits would speak through my aunts. Because the spiritual session seemed very real, we followed the advice that was given. GOD's Word warns us in 1 Peter 5: 8 to be sober and vigilant because your adversary the devil is like a hungry lion looking to devour you.

I remember that I lived a life of confusion because something inside me told me it was wrong to believe in those things. But when the spirits spoke and told the realities of our lives or showed their power - it brought much confusion to my life. They would send us to read Psalms in the Bible and tell us to go to Catholic mass on Sunday. Because of my lack of knowledge of the Word, I thought that it was from GOD. We would consult everything with the spirits. We would consult them about our work, our love life, health, money, and businesses. You name it, we sought the spirits for their wisdom.

Satan has many ways to destroy people, but his main weapons are deception and lies. JESUS said that false prophets would come in the last days and deceive many people with his great signs and miracles! In the middle of my confusion of believing in witches and sorcery, I met a guy that I was attracted to from the first time that I saw him. Without realizing it, the demons of witchcraft inside of me were attracted to the demons within this guy. He introduced himself to me and we started going out. He would mysteriously talk about himself as if he was hiding something about himself. I didn't know this man would end up ruining six years of my life!

With each of his visits to my house, pictures would disappear from my living room, and he would take more and more control of my life. If he did not call me, I would have anxiety attacks and my body would start to shake. This disappeared as soon as he would call me. It was something demonic. He would know my thoughts, my past, and my present, even when I hadn't shared with him! That brought even more confusion to my life. It turns out, this guy was a warlock! He cast a spell on me so I would not marry anyone else and never be happy unless I stayed with him. It got to a point where I felt like I was going crazy and I begged him not to be a part of my life, and I never wanted to see him again.

This started a psychological war between us. I wanted to escape from all this but in my strength, I could not. I turned to seek council with witches and warlocks because my loneliness was too great, and I wanted a way out! I started to bathe with honey, roses, cinnamon, sugar, herbs, light up candles, and many other things. I remember I even presented a dance to an image of a saint. Even though I was doing all these things, the spell from this guy grew stronger and stronger! I became the target and victim of married men. Partying and alcohol became my lifestyle, and I would go out with one guy after another, never being happy with anyone. My life was a total disaster.

Realizing that my involvement with witchcraft was not working, I turned to Catholicism. I prayed rosaries, hail Mary's, offering to saints, etc., and nothing! I felt trapped and as if I couldn't escape anymore so I kept partying and tried to fill the void with music. It was a momentary fix. I could be surrounded by people yet be tormented with a spirit of loneliness. The curse placed upon my life was so strong, it affected all my relationships, none of which were stable. I felt I had no purpose or destiny for my life. I felt like a failure and my hope was gone.

I left my country to start a new life. I thought I was escaping my past, however, I found myself living the vicious cycle that I wanted to get away from! I had carried all the baggage from my past with me. Unless you deal with the root of your issues, they will follow you wherever you go. The spell of witchcraft still had a grip on my life. I finally got to a place of total brokenness and screamed out to GOD to change my life. I knew He existed and asked Him to please give me a sign that He was real and to set me free! I told Him I couldn't go on anymore and surrendered my life to Him. My brokenness before the LORD was a turning point for my life. I found a God-fearing church, one that believed in deliverance. I went through a process, renouncing all the open doors of witchcraft and sorcery in my life. In His mercy, the LORD set me free and I am now serving the LORD and ministering to others so they can be free as well."

The Word of GOD tells us that we are not to practice witchcraft and magic. If you are trapped in witchcraft or under a curse that someone placed upon you, there is hope for you. JESUS paid the price for your sins and took every curse to the cross. Ask forgiveness, renounce the witchcraft, and break curses off your life in the name of JESUS. Ask HOLY SPIRIT to give you the power to overcome sin. If you went to a witch in the past for healing, protection, or direction for your life, renounce that as well, you have broken the first commandment.

You may not have directly been involved with witchcraft, but there may still be open doors that need to be renounced because of your ancestors or because of an individual from your past. I have ministered to individuals who never practiced witchcraft, but because a mother, grandfather, or another relative had, they renounced the generational curse and were delivered from the yoke of oppression that was on their life. GOD's commandments tell us He is visiting the iniquity of the fathers upon the children to the third and fourth generations of those who hate Him but will show mercy to those who love Him and keep His commandments (Exodus 20:4-6). Ask forgiveness on behalf of your past generations, renounce the spirit of witchcraft, cancel the curse off your life and your future generations, and rebuke the spirit of witchcraft. You will see the mercies of GOD come upon your life and the life of your generations to come.

After reading this chapter so far you may think you have never opened yourself to demonic behavior because no one in your generational line has practiced witchcraft. However, there may be subtle ways the enemy disguises himself to open doors of torment to your life. One subtle way is through the music you listen to.

What music do you listen to?

The following is a testimony of an individual called to be a worshipper, but Satan had another destiny for his life. As you read George's testimony you will see how Satan had him bound and how the influence of music affected his life.

"I started to play in a band because I wanted attention from my friends. I wanted to belong and be a part of something. I played music in the world for five years with a rock and roll band. I did not realize how demonic this type of music was. We used to drink and smoke marijuana while we were practicing. We even watched pornography while practicing and composing music. It came to the point that we were completely under the influence of alcohol and drugs and we couldn't do anything.

It was a very bad time for me when I was growing up. I moved here to the United States from Ecuador and almost got involved in a band in North Carolina, but that never took off. Although I was not a Christian, the hand of GOD was over my life because of the prayers of my wife. I moved from Charlotte, North Carolina to Kissimmee, Florida. That's when the transformation of my life began. My wife was a Christian and she would pray that my eyes could be open to the spiritual realm. Her prayers were answered because one day I saw demons in my house and as I lay in my bed, I felt a demon on top of me. Before this experience, I thought all the talk about demons was foolishness and I did not believe they were real. When this demon jumped on me, I got scared and I ran out of my house and went to some friends who were Christians. In the past, they would invite me to go to church, but I would never accept the offer. I knocked on their door and shared what I experienced. They said, "We were praying for this so you could see that Satan and his demons are real." That started the process of my Christian walk.

Once I realized the spiritual realm was real, it changed my whole perspective about the spiritual world. I repented of my sins and asked JESUS to come into my life. I realized my involvement with music, alcohol, and drugs opened doors in my life to the manifestation of demons. I didn't care what music my wife liked or disliked, I played what I loved and that was rock and roll music. Every time I would listen to music, it would entice me to buy alcohol or smoke marijuana. I realized my life was controlled by rock and roll music. Some people will say that it doesn't, it can't control you in that way, but it does. The problem is when you are addicted to worldly music, you are not even aware of it and the stronghold it has over your life. For me, the breakthrough came because of the strong faith of my wife, and because of the many people that were praying for me. I was so blinded by the fact that the spiritual realm was real. When my eyes were opened to the truth, I understood that JESUS gave me a calling to be a worshipper and the enemy was trying to steal that calling away from me.

As I began to observe the worship team playing for the LORD, I knew I wanted to be a part of that. When you are a worshipper and you have a calling on your life, the LORD puts that desire in you. I knew I had to go through a time of purification if I wanted to be on that altar serving the LORD. I had to go through a process of deliverance and detoxification of all the garbage that I had been listening to for so many years. I started my process of deliverance with the help of my pastor and a few brothers in the church. The first time my pastor came to my house, I was not expecting him to minister deliverance. But he sat down with my wife and me and began to pray, "Spirit of rock and roll music lose him." Something strange was happening, but I knew it was very real. I felt something quickly come out of my stomach. It came out as a growl. At this point in my life, I knew nothing about deliverance, but I knew what just happened was real.

After that night, I tried to listen to worldly music a few times, and each time I felt like I wanted to vomit. It was music, that in the past I really loved, but now it was making me sick to my stomach. I stopped completely listening to worldly music because I knew I had a calling in my life. For me, it was very hard because I couldn't go to sleep if I wasn't listening to rock and roll music. That is how addicted to the music I was. I had to play something loud and heavy to fall asleep. In my process of deliverance, I began to listen to soft Christian worship songs and that started changing me. That is how the LORD detoxed me from the worldly music that I used to listen to. Worship to me is a way of life. If you want to change from a musician to a true worshipper, you must give your all. There is no middle ground. That is what I did. You can't have one foot serving the LORD and the other foot serving the world. You must go all the way for JESUS and not be enticed by the things of the world."

You can see from George's testimony that rock and roll music opened the door to demonic influences of alcohol, drugs, and pornography. He did not believe demons existed until he had a personal encounter with one. His eyes were opened to the truth. Had the LORD not intervened in his life, I am sure a spirit of death would have ended his life.

What kind of music do you listen to? It's not just rock and roll music, it can also be worldly rap or worldly country music. Many of the lyrics have sexual connotations or even speak of death or suicide within the words. Many times, individuals sing songs because they sound good, without paying attention to what the lyrics say. These words then become ingrained into our subconscious mind. What thoughts do you struggle with? Could there be a connection between those tormenting thoughts and the type of music you listen to? That is why we should only be listening to Christian music that lifts and glorifies the name of JESUS. Ask the LORD to deliver you from worldly music. You can't listen to godly worship and worldly music and expect to hear clearly from the LORD. Ask GOD to purify you from the secular lyrics embedded in your subconscious mind.

It's only a game, or is it?

Video games have become such a popular form of entertainment. They are easily accessible and can be downloaded onto most electronic devices. If you are not careful, you could fall into a trap of the enemy. How do you spend your time? Are there any video games you are attracted to and can't seem to put down? A huge open door to Satan's demonic schemes is through what appears to be harmless games that entertain you for many hours of the day. What people don't realize is that many of the video games today are demonic and have underlying spirits of witchcraft, magic, violence, and death. You may have a teenager whose behavior has changed from a very sweet individual to one who has become rebellious and full of anger. You blame it on hormones and think this is normal for teenagers to go through, not realizing there is a spirit influencing his or her life from the video games being played.

Video games are very addictive. You don't have any time to serve the LORD or read His Word, but you can spend hours of the day playing video games. Satan is stealing your time, and you are falling prey to his subtle tactics. Satan may even have you blinded to the fact that most video games are demonic. You may think they are just for fun and entertainment. If this sounds like you, GOD wants to open your eyes to the spiritual truth. The following is a testimony of a young man who fell into the trap of the enemy and how the influence of video games controlled his life.

"On both sides of my family, there were problems with addictions. Just like drugs and alcohol, you can create an addiction to video games. I was eight years old when I received a Super Nintendo. I started playing it and liked the idea that your mind could be distracted from things. As a child, I felt very lonely because my parents were working all the time. I tried to fill that emptiness by playing video games. Playing video games was my escape from reality.

As I got older, my attraction to video games got worse by the day. I was addicted to all sorts of video games, the ones on the computers, X-Box, Play Station, every type of video game. I was very good at the games and my identity was developing around that. The most addicting ones for me were the role-playing games, the ones where you play the role of a character. You put your name to a character, and you start being that character. I began to identify with that character that I was playing with. Everyone was calling me and wanting to play with me because I was so good at it. That is the way the enemy lured me into his trap. My success in the games gave me the attention I desperately wanted for my life. I would play on an average of 3 to 7 hours a day so I could become very successful at the games.

Video games affected me in every area of my life. It affected my grades at the university and my relationship with my friends and family. Video games changed the way I related to people. Everything evolved around being in my room and playing video games. I didn't care about others, I just cared about spending time with the character I identified within the video game and being the best. I had escaped reality and became very isolated. It was a challenge for me to socialize with people. I had difficulty interacting with people because of the false identity I had in myself. In the game, I was the most successful person. But as soon as I quit playing the video game, I was this guy that had a pit of emptiness that could not be filled.

One demonic game that I was addicted to was World of Warcraft. This is a very popular video game amongst teenagers and young adults. This is a role-playing game where you create your character. The designers of World of Warcraft know the powers of darkness and created the game based on real demonic entities. They use demonic names from the Bible and other sources to create their characters. When you begin playing the World of Warcraft, they make you sign a contract electrically before you can create your character. As soon as you sign the contract unknowingly you align yourself in the spiritual realm and the game masters have authority over you. I was eager to sign the contract and created my character. I had many options to choose from. I could become a magician, a warlock, a witch, or a shaman (witch doctor), just to name a few. I chose to become a warlock and I declared this over my life many times.

The warlock's main ability was to place curses onto others. The warlock had special powers to cast fear or affliction onto their opponents. They could transform their opponents into demons. Every warlock had to make a blood covenant with a demon. I did this by doing some quests in the game and making alliances with the demons. I pronounced these covenants with my mouth and spoke them over my life. As a warlock, I cast spells onto others. I would play the game through Skype with my friends and as I played, I would say things like, "Let me curse this person with affliction or let me send a curse of agony to that person."

As I got deeper involved in the game, I made more covenants with other demons. I developed soul ties with the characters of the game. They became a part of me, and I loved how I felt. I became very trapped. People would ask who I was, and I proudly declared myself to be a warlock and that I could cast spells onto others.

My world of darkness brought such oppression over my life. I saw my friends accomplishing goals. They were getting awesome grades and finding good jobs. I was not dedicating the time I needed for my studies therefore my grades were average rather than making the A's and B's that I could do. I tried to quit playing video games several times. I would delete the games off my computer, but a day or two later I could not fight against the strong urge to download the games again. These addictive games had such a stronghold, I kept falling prey to their powers over my life.

I had confessed JESUS as my Savior, but my life was far from being a true Christian. I went to church for a few months but stopped going. My brother would share the Bible with me, and I began to listen, but at the same time I put up walls around me. My heart was not in JESUS, it was in the video games. I lost my relationship with my family and friends. I was constantly lying to my parents. It came to a point that I knew I could not continue in this lifestyle any longer. There was such emptiness and I realized the video games were not the solution. I was so oppressed and felt very desperate. I needed a drastic change in my life. I made a radical decision to give my life totally to JESUS. When I did that, the LORD sent Apostle Nebby Gomez to help break the demonic strongholds off my life.

I immediately started my deliverance process. It did not happen overnight. It was a process. I publicly confessed my sins and the LORD began to minister to my life. As I was prayed for, I started manifesting as if I was a warlock. I could feel wings on my back like the demons I made packs with. I renounced every soul tie and blood covenant that I had made and through the blood of JESUS they were broken. Every demon that entered through the video games was cast out of me. When they first started casting out the demons, they would not leave because I had made my room an altar for the demons. My desk and computer were filled with trash of video games and I had a Racer Nagar computer mouse which had a symbol of a snake on it. I destroyed the mouse along with all the video games, deleted all the demonic games off my computer. I erased every account I created and canceled every contract that I made so I could be completely free. As soon as I did this, all the demons lost their power and authority over my life. Through the power of the blood of JESUS, they were cast out of my life for good. The demons tried to come back, but because my decision for the LORD was sincere and from the heart, they no longer had any power over my life. Video games had control of my life for almost eight years. I thank the LORD for rescuing me out of the hands of Satan. I have surrendered my life to JESUS, and He has filled the emptiness I once had with His love, peace, and joy."

Video games are not just fun and games, most are demonic and full of darkness. Praise GOD Edwardo received the victory and found freedom through his faith and trust in JESUS. Don't be blinded by the enemy to think there is no harm in enjoying an innocent video game. It is true, some video games are harmless, but most of them are not. Use discernment and ask HOLY SPIRIT to show you if there is anything that could bring harm to your spiritual life through the playing of the video game. When you are walking in the light of JESUS, there is no middle ground. Light is light and darkness is darkness. If you are one of the millions of people who are trapped in video games, through the power of JESUS you can be set free from your addiction just as Edwardo was.

If your child plays with video games, research them to see if there is any form of demonic influence attached to them. If there is, your child needs to be ministered to. A word of caution: If you just take the games away from your children and tell them they can't play with them because they are evil without any explanation, they will manifest with rebellion. Before confronting them, pray and ask HOLY SPIRIT to give you wisdom in how to minister to your child(ren). Sit down and view portions of the video games with them, point out the evil, and show them in the Word of GOD that it is wrong. Make sure you pray, apply the blood of JESUS, and ask the LORD to protect you before watching them. Open the Bible and have them read for themselves what GOD's Word says about these things. This will allow HOLY SPIRIT to open your child's eyes of understanding, speak to his/her heart, and bring the conviction of sin to their life. It is only then that they will have the desire to stop playing.

It's not just video games we need to be careful of. There are card and board games that are just as demonic. Pokémon has become so popular. Did you know Pokémon was short for "pocket monster? Playing games like the Ouija board can also open the door to spiritual torment.

I remember as a child playing the Ouija board out of curiosity. I had gone over to a neighbor's house and a few of the young children were playing and I began to participate with them. At the time I did not realize I was playing with a spirit board. I don't remember the question I asked, but I do remember the answer it gave through the planchette (moveable indicator). The spirit behind that spirit board moved the indicator to spell out the word "death". After that happened, I was terrified, and I ran home. For days I had nightmares. Throughout my teenage years, I suffered from depression. I had no reason to be depressed. I was making good grades, involved in sports, and was quite popular in school. Yet I felt this void in my life and couldn't explain what that void was, nor could I explain the reason for the oppression I struggled with. In my early twenties, I tried to commit suicide by taking an overdose of Valium. My roommate in college found me unconscious and sought medical help. The LORD had mercy on me and spared my life, even though I was not a Christian at that time.

A few years later a coworker began talking to me about her church and the things of GOD. She had such a joy about herself, I wanted that joy and asked her how I could receive it. She began sharing the love of JESUS, the only one who could bring true joy to my life. I asked JESUS to become my Savior and LORD of my life. Making that decision changed my life in many ways, however, I still struggled with depression. It wasn't until years later when I heard about deliverance and went through that process that I found my freedom. I asked for forgiveness and renounced witchcraft and any demon that entered through playing the Ouija board, including the spirit of death. I was set free from oppression, depression, and all thoughts of suicide. I am so thankful to GOD I have YESHUA in my life who gives me victory over death. That was over forty years ago, and I have not had one suicidal thought since my deliverance. Little did I know about His plans for my life, but I give thanks to the LORD I am alive to testify of His goodness and walk in the prophetic journey He has for my life. May GOD receive all the glory!

Seek HOLY SPIRIT for discernment before buying any video games or any other form of entertainment. Ask the LORD to show you if there are any spirits associated with them that could open the door to Satan's schemes. You may think it's just fun and games, but sooner or later the enemy comes to collect taxes over your life. Ask the LORD to show you if you have any open doors from games you have played with in the past.

Is watching television harmful?

Television is one of Satan's means of entertaining the works of the flesh. Over the past decades, television programs have become more sensual and demoralizing. All sorts of ungodly behaviors are broadcasted, and individuals have become immune to them.

What television programs do you watch? What do you allow your children to watch? Have you considered the spirits behind those television programs? Another tool Satan uses to lure people into captivity is through television and movies. Many parents use the television as a babysitter. They allow their children to watch shows and cartoons without paying attention to what they are seeing. Many programs children watch, including cartoons, contain witchcraft, magic, and violence. Children become insensitive to these and out of curiosity want to try it out for themselves. Children are great imitators, and they will mimic what they see. Do you want your children experimenting with witchcraft? Many teenagers are being drawn into occultism practices. Anger and rebellion are also prevalent in children and teenagers. Is it any wonder with the violence they observe on television and video games? You may not think toddlers are too young to be affected, but they are.

"My husband enjoyed watching World Wrestling Entertainment. When my son Jason was about two years of age, he began watching wrestling with his father. Every Saturday evening, they sat in front of the television to watch the show. As time passed Jason began acting very hostile. How could such a young child be filled with such anger? He used to roll his eyes like Undertaker, one of the wrestlers. We realized a spirit of anger was tormenting our son and the open door to that anger was from allowing him to watch the wrestling program on the television. As parents, we became very concerned because we didn't realize the exposure and harm we had brought to our son. We thought it was only a show and nothing else. We learned about deliverance and laid hands on Jason and in the name of JESUS rebuked the spirit of anger out of him. We also asked forgiveness to the LORD for allowing our son to watch the wrestling program. Thank the LORD my son was set free, and he no longer has any signs of anger, hostility, nor rebellion. We learned a very valuable lesson."

The impact of television has the potential to pollute your mind and your emotions. The next time you sit down to watch television ask yourself this question, "What kind of seeds are being planted in my mind if I watch this program?

Is there a hidden agenda?

The word occult comes from the Latin word *occultus* which means hidden from sight, secret, or esoteric (mysterious)[1]. Many occult practices appear genuine but have a hidden agenda. William Schnoebelen, an ex-32nd degree Mason exposes the truth about Freemasonry. This international fraternal is a secret society that appears to be a Christian organization, but those who reach higher levels know differently. Unknown to most Masons, there is an occult side to Masonry. It is at levels in Masonry that most Masons never get to.[2] The Masonic temple is a temple of witchcraft, explains Schnoebelen. Veiled within its symbols are the deities and even the working tools of witchcraft.[3] If you confront a Mason with the truth, they will usually manifest with anger and say it isn't so. Unless HOLY SPIRIT reveals the reality of its origin to them, they are spiritual blinded to the truth. There are many dangerous oaths that candidates of Freemasonry recite, not realizing they are placing curses upon themselves. One example is binding themselves to the organization and having their throat cut, the tongue tore out, and the body buried if one violates the obligation.[4] Unknowingly they bind themselves to this occultic society and bring a curse of death if they abandon it.

Many evangelical churches have individuals on their governing board who are members of Freemasonry. Where is the discernment? Is it any wonder many churches today lack the presence and power of HOLY SPIRIT? If you would like to learn more about the hidden agenda of Freemasonry, I highly suggest reading the book "Masonry Beyond the Light" by William Schnoebelen.

Is there any harm to engaging in martial arts?

There has been a growing trend of martial arts over the past two decades. Many see martial arts as a form of exercise or self-defense and do not see the potential dangers associated with karate and other forms of martial arts. People blindly see Yoga as a form of relaxation. All martial arts trace their roots back to the false religions of Hinduism and Buddhism. They teach that what is known as GOD by the western Christian world, is an energy force or great spirit and through proper techniques, meditation, spiritual exercises, and lifestyle, we may all become one with this divine energy.[5]

Martial artists train in deep meditation and breathing techniques to open the mind to the influence of the spirit world. The ability to control one's breathing is used to enter an altered state of consciousness. This type of meditation opens the mind to spirits of darkness. Martial arts also involve the use of Chi and Qi which are sources of demonic powers in the traditional Chinese culture. These powers can surface very suddenly and violently in the individual's every-day life.

Many see martial arts as training focusing on athletic skills. Many schools advertise after-school martial arts programs and encourage children to participate in them. The spiritual component of martial arts must be considered before getting your child involved. Do you want to expose your child to these spirits of darkness? If your child is participating in martial arts and is demonstrating hostile behavior, it is highly possible the root of his aggressiveness is a spirit of aggression coming from Chi or Qi.

What are you embracing?

New Age religion is not new, it has been around for centuries. It combines occult practices, self-help, holistic medicines, and astrology. New Age tolerates most forms of religions and beliefs, but directly blasphemies the doctrine of Judeo-Christian beliefs. They refute the belief that JESUS is the only way to eternal salvation. New Age believers think GOD is in everything and everything is God. They think that the universe, life, and matter were not created by GOD but are God. They also believe man is God, and salvation is self-achieved when you realize your natural godlikeness and goodness. This is the same lie Satan told Eve in the Garden when he said, "you will be like GOD". New Age is far from biblical truth. Here is Tabitha's testimony of how deceptive it can be.

"Growing up I always felt sad, unloved, and betrayed. My parents gave me up for adoption and I never felt good enough or loved by my adoptive parents. I was often depressed and suicidal. I struggled to find my identity. Part of my childhood was going to a catholic school. It was there, at the age of 13, that I was exposed to Silva's mind control. This mind control incorporates a variety of occultic practices such as clairvoyance and other psychic abilities, guides, visualization, and New Age. It emphasized self and looking inward to teach you how to be better and the idea that the mind is god and that we can accomplish anything we set our minds to do.

I immediately chose to embrace this because I wanted to control people's minds and make them love me. I was fascinated with the psychic and wanted to learn how to invite counselors or psychic guides to help me resolve all my problems. Little did I realize that I was being led down the wrong path. I started using mind control on individuals, sending them messages to accept and love me, and to do things they did not care to do. One time I was running late for an important meeting and was in the middle of a lot of traffic. I began to send messages to the mind of people that were driving in front of me to move over. To my surprise, people started to move over and when I would pass them, they would look at me with an astonished face, wondering why they moved over in the first place.

Through mind control, I learned to concentrate and let go of all my feelings and emotions and mentally freeze my pain away. I used this method when I was giving birth to my daughter, I started to freeze my body mentally and I gave birth without any pain. You might say well that is great, but this is not accepted by GOD because I was using powers that were not from Him to take my pain away.

Another thing that I would do is read and talk to people's minds. There were times when my husband was sleeping, and I wanted him to wake up. I would stand in the doorway of our bedroom and send messages to his mind that it was time to get up. He would awaken, half asleep and not wanting to get up. He would get so upset with me because he knew I sent messages to his mind to wake up.

Out of curiosity my husband and son began to play with mind control. My husband would tell my son to say the number he was thinking of, my son would focus for a moment and then guess it correctly. Then he would do the same to his father. They would play back and forth, but it wasn't a game. They were falling into a game of mind control just by innocently playing this game.

I gained the ability to move things from one place to another just from concentrating. I got more involved with mind control and this led me to go deeper into New Age and Yoga. I was trying to control my life not realizing that Satan's major focus was to divert my heart away from the worship of the one and only true GOD. He enticed me with the suggestions of power, self-realization, and spiritual enlightenment and I fell for it.

With New Age, I started collecting stones and believing that if I wore them as a bracelet or on a chain, they would bring healing or good luck.

I was so enticed by the psychic that I started visiting sorcerers to have them pray for my back, neck, and shoulders because I was having pain. They laid hands on me, passed leaves over me, and declared the pain to be gone. But instead of getting better, the pain got worse. I decided not to waste my time and chose not to go back. But still, I was blinded to the open door I created in my life.

A year later we moved, and the LORD led me to a church that believes in deliverance. Today, I am grateful to GOD that He has set me free of all these evil paths which were leading me to my spiritual death. I have repented, renounced, and rebuked all this out of my life. I now only worship the KING of kings and the LORD of lords. He has given me my identity in Him. I now have a Father that loves me and cares for me, the one that I can turn to when I am in need. He has given me the revelation that I never received through any of the psychic methods I used in the past. If the enemy has deceived you and you are trapped in his schemes, run from this, you are in danger. I invite you to give your life to JESUS and repent."

Tabitha was searching to fill a void in her life. Every religion she tried could not fill that void. It wasn't until she gave her life to JESUS that she felt the love she had been searching for and she finally realized her identity came through her relationship with her LORD and Savior. You may be experiencing a void in your life. Don't try to fill that emptiness with worldly things. Allow JESUS to fill you with His love.

Don't embrace any form of religion or practice that is contrary to the Word of GOD. They will lead you down a path of destruction. There are many religions and practices not mentioned in this book. Ask HOLY SPIRIT to show you if you have any open doors from religious practices from your past. If you have followed a religion that denies the deity of JESUS, you need to renounce that religion and rebuke every spirit attached to it.

What spirit is behind your holiday?

I'm sure you have heard the expression, "Let's get into the spirit of Christmas." But do you understand the true meaning behind this phrase? If I were to ask you, "What is the spirit of Christmas?", your answer may be shopping and buying gifts, buying a Christmas tree, and decorating it, or celebrating the birth of JESUS. I believe one of the greatest deceptions people have fallen into is the belief that Christmas is about celebrating the birth of JESUS and Easter is about celebrating His death and resurrection. I was blinded by these lies for many years and taught my children to celebrate these traditions as well. Tradition is very strong in this nation and many times we celebrate without understanding the root of what we are celebrating. Do not allow your traditions to close your eyes to what GOD wants to reveal to you today. Ask HOLY SPIRIT to speak to you and bring revelation as you read the scriptures that support what I am writing. Your decision to believe or not believe should be based on GOD's Word and not on your customs and family traditions. The Word of GOD tells us that people perish because of lack of knowledge (Hosea 4:6) and the truth shall set you free (John 8:32). I pray HOLY SPIRIT will bring the revelation and reveal the truth to your heart.

If a feast was to be observed by GOD's people, GOD always gave clear instructions on how to celebrate it. Leviticus 23 lists the feasts of the LORD and gives clear directions to follow. The feasts that are mentioned here are not the feasts of the Jews, they are GOD's feasts.

"Speak to the children of Israel and say to them: The feasts of the LORD, which you shall proclaim to be holy convocations, these are My feasts."

- Leviticus 23:2

If Christmas was from GOD, why is the fruit of celebrating it opposite from the fruit of HOLY SPIRIT? Have you noticed how greed is so prevalent? Just watch people's behavior during the Black Friday shopping spree. Christmas is a time of year when ungrateful people open presents, only to be dissatisfied with what they receive. Covetousness overtakes people, and they spend way more than they can afford, only to have credit cards charged to the max. According to the National Institute of Health, there is a Christmas holiday effect on mortality which spikes during this season of the year. Possible explanations include emotional stress associated with the holiday, changes in diet, and alcohol consumption.[6] Greed, covetousness, depression, gluttony, and alcoholism are all fruit of celebrating a tradition established by man.

When you celebrate the feasts of the LORD, you experience the fruit of HOLY SPIRIT in your life. Celebrating the LORD's feasts brings great joy knowing your sins are forgiven. Oppression and the bondage of sin are broken, and the joy of the LORD enters your heart. You don't have to worry about credit card debt, your gift of eternal life is free, JESUS paid the price in full. Halloween is about skulls, skeletons, and cemeteries. When you celebrate Halloween, you are celebrating death and open the door to fear and torment. Children are traumatized when they see others dressed up as Dracula, witches, and other demonic costumes. Eating all the sugar from candy used to celebrate these holidays leads to sugar addiction, obesity, and diseases such as diabetes. When you celebrate the feasts of the LORD, you celebrate life. The weight of sin is lifted from you and peace enters your heart. You crave the things of the LORD which brings healing through the blood of YESHUA.

If you want to truly celebrate the birth, life, death, and resurrection of JESUS you need to see Him as revealed through the Feasts of the LORD and how He is the fulfillment of these feasts. Celebrate what GOD has called holy, don't give in to the ways of men, and follow the traditions you have been taught since you were young. Nowhere in the Bible are Christmas, Easter, Valentine's Day, or Halloween ever mentioned. Without realizing it, you are mixing JESUS, the root of your faith, with another spirit that has nothing to do with HOLY SPIRIT. Unfortunately, your spiritual life will suffer the consequences of your sin.

"Why do you also transgress the commandment of God because of your tradition?"
- Matthew 15:3

Beware lest anyone cheat you through philosophy and empty deceit, according to the tradition of men, according to the basic principles of the world, and not according to Christ.
- Colossians 2:8

Both scriptures give a warning not to follow the traditions of men, but rather the Word of GOD. Outwardly, celebrating Christmas has the appearance of being good. After all, you are celebrating the birthday of JESUS, but are you? Luke 2 gives the account of the birth of JESUS. Joseph and Mary were in Bethlehem because of the census ordered by Caesar Augustus. While there she gave birth to JESUS.

So it was, that while they were there, the days were completed for her to be delivered. And she brought forth her firstborn Son, and wrapped Him in swaddling clothes, and laid Him in a manger because there was no room for them in the inn. Now there were in the same country shepherds living out in the fields, keeping watch over their flock by night.
- Luke 2:6-8

Shepherds were tending their sheep in the fields at the time that JESUS was born. December is very rainy and cold in Israel, sometimes cold enough to snow. It is too cold for shepherds to keep their flocks out at night grazing in winter. During the winter they are taken into shelters where it is warmer. The sheep are released into the fields in the early spring and remain outside until mid or late October when the weather gets cold. This supports the fact that JESUS was not born in December, but rather in a warmer month.

You may have been taught that wise men came and gave gifts to baby JESUS. Matthew 2 gives the account of when the wise men came to Jerusalem saying, "Where is He who has been born King of the Jews?" The wise men were led by a star to find where JESUS was. They didn't find a baby in a manger. He was a young child. That is why Herod had all male children two years and younger killed because JESUS was a threat to his kingship. If JESUS had been a newborn baby, Herod would have ordered only infants to be killed. But instead, he ordered two years and younger to be killed, supporting the fact that JESUS was approximately two years of age when the wise men arrived.

Nowhere in the Bible will you find the disciples, nor the early church, celebrating His birth. If GOD wanted you to celebrate it, He would have said so in His Word and He would have given clear instructions on how to celebrate it. Jim Stanley, the pastor from Passion of Truth Ministries, has a YouTube video called *Truth or Tradition*. The video goes into detail discussing the facts from recorded history and the Word of GOD to teach you the truth. I highly suggest you watch it for more insight into this topic.

Who are your celebrations pleasing?

Some people light candles on a birthday cake and sing Happy Birthday to JESUS, thinking it is bringing honor to Him. They are doing it from the pureness of heart, but does that make it right? It's not about what you want to celebrate, it's what GOD wants you to celebrate. How would you feel if someone you love insists on celebrating your birthday, not on your actual birthday, but the birthday of an ex? Not only that, but they also celebrate in a way contrary to your liking. How would you feel? I'm sure you would feel offended.

When you associate the birth of JESUS with Christmas, that is exactly what you are doing. You observe your traditions and what you think will honor GOD instead of obeying His truth and doing what pleases His heart. Although you are celebrating with a sincere heart, by celebrating Christmas and Easter, you are worshiping JESUS through pagan holidays. Search the Scriptures for yourself. See if you can find anywhere in the Bible where Christmas or Easter is mentioned and observed. You won't find it! Why, because they are not from GOD! However, you will find the feasts of the LORD which He instructs you to observe. Each of these feasts has a profound meaning and point you to YESHUA.

Are you willing to break from tradition?

Once my husband and I gained the revelation of the pagan roots of Christmas, HOLY SPIRIT brought conviction to our hearts. We asked the LORD for forgiveness and renounced any spirit that may have entered through celebrating this holiday. We chose not to celebrate Christmas ever again. We sat down with our family members and explained why we made the decision. The choice was easy, but it came with a price. Our families were quite upset with us and didn't agree with our decision, but that didn't sway us in any way. We chose to please the heart of GOD rather than the hearts of our family. As the years have passed, our family members respect our decision even though they still celebrate Christmas. We will gather, not to celebrate Christmas, but instead gather around the table, enjoying a special dinner and celebrate family. We don't judge them for all the festivities of Christmas. After all, until we gained the revelation, we celebrated too. Our prayer is that HOLY SPIRIT will bring revelation to their lives, just as He did to us.

> *"Now, therefore, fear the LORD, serve Him in sincerity and in truth, and put away the gods which your fathers served on the other side of the River and in Egypt. And if it seems evil to you to serve the LORD, choose for yourselves this day whom you will serve, whether the gods which your fathers served that were on the other side of the River or the gods of the Amorites, in whose land you dwell. But as for me and my house, we will serve the LORD."*
>
> *- Joshua 24:14-15*

Whatever holiday or tradition you celebrate, search the Internet to find its origin and see if it is contrary to the Word of GOD. You will be surprised to find there is a false god or goddess behind most of the traditional holidays you celebrate. And behind those false gods and goddesses are unclean spirits. You cannot mix something unclean with HOLY SPIRIT which lives inside of you. Is it any wonder why you sometimes feel so distant from GOD? It is up to you, you make the decision but just as Joshua chose for him and his family, as for me and my house, we will serve the LORD.

> "But the hour is coming, and now is, when the true worshipers will worship the Father in spirit and truth; for the Father is seeking such to worship Him. God is SPIRIT and those who worship Him must worship in spirit and truth."
>
> - John 4:23-24

When you break the first commandment, it will affect your relationship with GOD. Often it manifests itself as oppression. You may feel spiritually dry, struggle to read His Word, have difficulty praying, and feel distant from GOD. There may even be a spirit of death over you because of open doors to your past that have not been dealt with. Unless you close the doors to your former religions and demonic activities, these symptoms will linger. Don't allow the enemy to steal the beautiful blessings the LORD has for your life as you draw closer to Him.

Questions for Thought
1. What ways of seeking counsel are forbidden according to the Word of GOD?
2. Do you know the origin of the holidays you celebrate?
3. Why should you be careful of the music you listen to?
4. Why are most video games harmful?

Are you ready to let go of anything from your past that hinders your walk with GOD? To begin your process of deliverance, refer to Section 3, First Commandment. You will find a list of underlying spirits that may be operating, causing you to break the first commandment. There are also prayer guides to assist you. Let's get started with your process of deliverance!

Chapter 9
WHAT IS YOUR PASSION?

Commandment Two
"You shall not make for yourself a carved image – any
likeness of anything that is in heaven above, or that is in the
earth beneath, or that is in the water under the earth; you
shall not bow down to them nor serve them. For I, the LORD
your God, am a jealous God, visiting the iniquity of the
fathers upon the children to the third and fourth generations
of those who hate Me, but showing mercy to thousands, to
those who love Me and keep My commandments."
- Exodus 20:4-6

The last chapter you read about whom you should worship and the spirits behind false gods. This chapter is about what you worship. When you first look at this commandment, the letter of this Law is obvious. You are not to make any carved images, bow down to them, nor worship them. Yet many are doing the exact opposite of GOD's Word. Religious people bowing down to statues, worshipping animals, carving totem poles, or lighting candles and praying to saints. Some put their trust in carrying a rabbit's foot for good luck rather than putting their trust in GOD. Many people, cities, and nations are under a curse because of their pagan roots. That is why many countries struggle with oppression, poverty, and mortality.

Anything made to be a representation of a god is idolatry and it opens the door to spiritual adultery. Idols such as statues, relics, good luck charms, and souvenirs are open doors to bring torment and they must be removed from your life. GOD is a jealous GOD visiting the iniquity of the fathers to four generations. He does not want to share His deity with anyone or anything, and that is exactly what you are doing when you pray to the Virgin Mary or a shrine of a saint.

> For there is one God and one Mediator between God and men, the Man Christ Jesus.
> - 1 Timothy 2:5

Who are you praying to?

Many individuals have erected altars in their homes or yards and lifted their prayers to the statues of false gods or saints, not realizing it is an offense to GOD. You should not try to reach the throne of grace in this manner. Your relationship with GOD should not be through statues and other graven images. This sin is addressed throughout the Bible and GOD commands those altars to be destroyed. No image can come close to the likeness of GOD. GOD is SPIRIT and we must worship Him in spirit and truth.

Your hope cannot be through religious rituals, prayers, and deeds. Exchange your religion for a personal relationship with JESUS through HOLY SPIRIT. Your hope is in JESUS the Messiah who died and resurrected. He is no longer on the cross. It is through His precious blood that you can obtain salvation, deliverance, and healing.

Who comes first in your life?

The Spirit of this Law goes much deeper than the letter of this Law. Idolatry extends beyond the worship of idols, images, and false gods. GOD needs to be first in your life. You were created to worship Him. You have free will to choose who and what you worship. If you place anything or anyone above Him, that object or person becomes an idol in your life. Your husband, wife, and children can potentially become an idol if you are not careful. JESUS warns us about this in the book of Luke.

"If anyone comes to Me and does not hate his father and mother, wife and children, brothers and sisters, yes, and his own life also, he cannot be My disciple."

- Luke 14:26

To understand what JESUS is saying, you need to go back to the original Greek. The Greek word used in the above scripture for the word hate means to love less[1]. If you take it back to the original, it would read something like this: "If anyone comes to Me and does not love his father and mother, wife and children, brother and sister, yes, and his own life also less than me, he cannot be My disciple. Your first love should be JESUS. He doesn't want a second place in your heart. Guard your heart so that you do not elevate anyone above GOD. No one should come between you and Him, not even your spouse and children. Never place your spouse on a pedestal, thinking he/she is the greatest and can do no wrong. Are your actions pleasing GOD or pleasing man? When you are more concerned about pleasing people rather than pleasing GOD, then He is not first in your heart.

What are you storing up?

Materialism and wealth can be a blessing. However, they can become sinful if you put your trust in them and allow greed and selfishness to settle in your heart. In Luke 12 JESUS speaks a parable about the rich fool. The rich man filled his barns and had no room for his crops. Rather than sharing his wealth, he chose to keep it for himself.

"So, he said, 'I will do this: I will pull down my barns and build greater, and there I will store all my crops and my goods. And I will say to my soul, "Soul, you have goods laid up for many years; take your ease; eat, drink, and be merry."' But God said to him, 'Fool! This night your soul will be required of you; then whose will those things be which you have provided?'"

- Luke 12:18-20

89

The rich man was hoarding his goods and only thinking of himself. He lost the blessing of helping others in need. He was proud of his accomplishments and celebrated his success. Selfishness and pride are sins and are the fruit of idolatry. Don't let your bank account become an idol.

> "Do not lay up for yourselves treasures on earth, where moth and rust destroy and where thieves break in and steal; but lay up for yourselves treasures in heaven, where neither moth nor rust destroys and where thieves do not break in and steal. For where your treasure is, there your heart will be also."
> - Matthew 6:19-21

What else can be an idol?

Does your job come before GOD? Your job could be an idol in your life. Aaron made this mistake and the LORD allowed his job to be taken away.

"At the age of eighteen, I joined the United States Marine Corps. It was and will always be one of the best decisions that I ever made. I will never down talk or hurt the image of an organization that has assisted me in being the man that I have become. Nevertheless, the Marine Corps has one drawback that affected my life negatively. It instills into you a mentality or mindset that is very prideful. The train of thought drilled into you while earning the title Marine is one where you are taught that the Marine Corps comes first above everything else. Of course, the Corps does not imply that you should put them above GOD or your family. However, I am very passionate, dedicated, and compulsive. When you combine these traits, situations can be tough to overcome.

During my time in the military, I had the utmost privilege of serving my country twice overseas while assisting in different military operations. I loved all the glamor and glory that came with being a United States Marine. It soon became my only priority in life. In the past, people would always fail me for one reason or another. I always used to think that I couldn't trust people, but the Marine Corps will never fail me.

The Marine Corps became a god in my eyes. I thought it was all I needed in life and pursued this as my career. I believed they would always be there for me and that my hard work would be rewarded with accomplishments that would make my family proud and make me feel complete and successful. At one point in my career, I became a recruiter for the marines. I flourished in this position and received promotions that were well above my peers. At this time, there was nothing that I loved more than the Marines.

Everything in my life was as I had planned. Everything was going my way. I was a successful recruiting station commander, I was financially stable, in a great relationship, and close to home. Then from one day to the next, it was all jeopardized. I got a new commander who came in and told me that my request for a permanent duty station was not going to happen. His decision affected me dramatically and I felt betrayed and all my hard work had been taken for granted.

I decided to retire from the Marine Corps and honestly, it was the hardest decision I ever made. However, my compulsive nature and passion would not let me overcome what had happened. Instead of remembering all the great times and the triumphs, I would only focus on the negative. I began to have cycles of depression and compulsive behaviors because of what happened in the Marine Corps. I knew my only hope was to surrender my life to GOD. I asked forgiveness to the LORD for my idolatry towards the Marines and entered a deliverance process. I asked the LORD to free me of every stronghold that was upon my life because of my sin. The process took over four months of renouncing and rebuking the military mindset. Slowly but surely, my way of thinking was transformed. I drew closer to GOD, my family, my church family, and even proposed to and married my wife who has stood beside me through those difficult times.

Looking back, I can see the LORD's hand involved in my retiring from the Marines. Without the process of deliverance, the weight on my shoulders would never have been lifted. The idolatry and disappointment with the Marines would have taken me into a downward spiral of depression. I now see clearer, GOD and my family is my priority, work isn't who I am, it is only a part of what I am and what GOD wants me to be."

Even sports and athletes can become an idol if you are not careful. If you are spending hours of your time in front of a television watching racing, football, soap operas, etc. yet spending little or no time in the Word of GOD or praying, that sport or television program has become an idol. Here is Mike's testimony.

"I have always been a football fan, and every football fan will tell you that the NFL playoffs and the Super Bowl are the high holy days of the football season. As far back as I can remember the postseason was the days that I would sit in front of the television with family and friends and party. The food and drinks were great, especially the cold beer. There was so much excitement about having your home team in the game, rooting for them to win. And, when they made it to the Super Bowl, the pride would overflow to screaming and hollering. As the big day approached, I would listen and view every report on the big game. On game day I took pride in giving the latest stats on players and coaches to those attending the game. Those were the days, or so I thought.

When I become a Christian, the party went from eating and drinking to just watching. For years, I would miss church, just to be able to watch the Super Bowl game. The Super Bowl was a priority in my life, nothing could stop me from watching it, so I thought. However, something began to change in me, it just didn't seem right to miss church to watch games that had no eternal value. The LORD started working on me and I started to feel convicted because I was putting the Super Bowl before my LORD. I realized that I was breaking GOD's commandment. I had to restore the heart of GOD, but how? Don't get me wrong, watching the Super Bowl is not a sin but putting anything before GOD is. I made a conscientious decision and decided to honor GOD rather than men. On the very next Super Bowl Sunday, I went to church to honor, worship, and praise my GOD. My LORD was waiting for me. I received the gift of tongues of HOLY SPIRIT that night. My obedience was rewarded with the gift of tongues. Hallelujah, hallelujah."

Mike will never forget his experience with the LORD that day. GOD supernaturally met him, and it transformed his life. He still talks about it today. When you place GOD first in your life, He will reward you with many spiritual blessings.

What idol are you bowing down to?

In the last chapter, you read about the spirit of Christmas. I want to address the idolatry that is found in the celebration of Christmas as well. Part of the tradition of celebrating Christmas is putting up a Christmas tree. This is a deep-rooted tradition. What does GOD's Word say about it?

> *Thus says the LORD: "Do not learn the way of the Gentiles; do not be dismayed at the signs of heaven, for the Gentiles are dismayed at them. For the customs of the peoples are futile; for one cuts a tree from the forest, the work of the hands of the workman, with the ax. They decorate it with silver and gold; they fasten it with nails and hammers so that it will not topple."*
>
> *- Jeremiah 10:2-4*

What does this sound like to you? Although Jeremiah was addressing the customs of that time, this can easily be applied to the custom of bringing in an evergreen tree into the home and decorating it for Christmas. When you follow the traditions of your ancestors without a Biblical root it is futile, it's worthless! I used to love celebrating Christmas and decorating the Christmas tree. Christmas wasn't Christmas without a Christmas tree. It was a deep-rooted tradition in my family and the family of my husband.

> *"You shall not plant for yourself any tree, as a wooden image, near the altar which you build for yourself to the LORD your God."*
>
> *- Deuteronomy 16:21*

You are the temple of the living GOD and celebrating JESUS with a Christmas tree should not be near the heart of a Christian. By placing gifts under the tree, you are bowing down to an idol without even realizing it. That may not have been your intention. However, it doesn't make it right.

GOD is a jealous GOD and is very serious about idolatry. He sees it as spiritual adultery and will punish it to the third and fourth generation. Close every opened door to idolatry and put the LORD in His rightful place, first in your heart. This will open the door for the mercy of the LORD to be upon you.

Questions for Thought

1. Why is it wrong to make carved images?
2. What does GOD consider an idol?
3. In what ways can we take away GOD's glory and praise?
4. What does JESUS mean when He said you cannot be His disciple if anyone does not hate his family or himself? (Luke 14:26)

Has the Word of GOD brought conviction of sin? Let's remove the idolatry from your life and place GOD above everything else. Refer to Section 3, Second Commandment to continue your process of deliverance.

Chapter 10
ARE YOU GUILTY?

Commandment Three
*"You shall not take the name of the LORD your God in
vain, for the LORD will not hold him guiltless who takes
His name in vain."*
- Exodus 20:7

One of the most important ways to respect GOD is found in
the third commandment. You are commanded by GOD to
honor and respect His name. That is why you see GOD, JESUS,
HOLY SPIRIT, and any reference to Him capitalized throughout
this book. It is a form of reverence. GOD is a holy God.
Everything about Him is holy. Even His name is holy. It is sacred
and GOD will hold you accountable if you misuse or profane His
name.

> *"You shall not profane My holy name, but I will be hallowed
> among the children of Israel. I am the LORD who sanctifies
> you, who brought you out of the land of Egypt, to be your
> God: I am the LORD."*
> *- Leviticus 22:32*

Why do you think GOD feels so strongly about His name?

Why do you think GOD feels so strongly about His name? It is
because a name reflects who you are. It is a part of your identity.
How would you feel if someone were to disrespect your name,

especially a name which defamed your character? You want people to associate something positive with your name, not something vulgar or demeaning. Today there is a big concern about identity theft. How much more should we be concerned about stealing the identity of the LORD! GOD's name is the divine nature of who He is. GOD is holy, He is all-loving, He is the absolute truth, He is righteous and faithful. These are just a few expressions of the true nature of His character. Each name used in the Bible describes one of His attributes. For example, Jehovah-Rapha, the LORD that heals.

The more you come to know who GOD is, the more you understand His character. Observing the third commandment is essential in developing a proper relationship with GOD. Satan knows the power behind the name of JESUS. That is why the enemy of your soul will do everything in his power to stop you from blessing the LORD. When you take the name of GOD in vain, you are robbing yourself of tremendous blessings and are opening the door to allow Satan to go before your Heavenly FATHER and bring an accusation against you.

What is vanity?

We are instructed in the third commandment not to use GOD's name in vain. What does it mean to take His name in vain? Webster's Dictionary defines vain as having no real value, idle, worthless, marked by futility. It also means unsuccessful and useless.[1] It is a privilege to use GOD's name and we cannot take that privilege lightly. Unfortunately, the name of GOD is carelessly thrown around and His character is belittled. Thoughtlessly using GOD's name is saying that GOD has little value. GOD demands that you respect His name and when you use it, it must be with a sincere heart and accurately represent Him as a holy GOD.

How do you use GOD's name in vain? The most obvious way of breaking the third commandment is through profanity, freely using His name or the name of JESUS in anger. Children of all ages have learned from their parents to dishonor GOD and frequently use His name in vain without an understanding of what they are doing. Out of hostility or resentment, people will mix the name of GOD with profane words. "G-d damn you". They are using GOD's name to bring condemnation to another person's life. This is not the nature of GOD. He is a merciful GOD and does not want to see your life cursed. If you are a Christian, take off the old nature and walk in the new. If you had a habit of cursing before you became a Christian, ask HOLY SPIRIT to give you the power to overcome that habit.

Are you guilty?

Taking GOD's name in vain is common practice today. We casually use His name in everyday conversation. Most people don't even realize they are doing it because it is a natural expression for them. How many times have you heard or used the expression "Oh my G_D" or "J__C__" when you are upset? You use this expression carelessly as a simple response and in doing so you are using the name of GOD in vain. You are bringing a curse upon yourself and your generations.

> *"And now, O priests, this commandment is for you. If you will not take it to heart, to give glory to My name," says the LORD of hosts, "I will send a curse upon you, and I will curse your blessings. Yes, I have cursed them already, because you do not take it to heart. Behold, I will rebuke your descendants."*
> *- Malachi 2:1-3*

How many blessings have you missed out on because of your guilt? If you are not walking in the blessings of GOD, the root may be that you, your parents, or your grandparents have taken GOD's name in vain.

GOD's name is often used in taking oaths with expressions such as "I swear to G_D". In the Old Testament swearing by GOD's name was meaningful. Today, this is no longer the case. When one uses GOD's name in an oath and then lies, he has misused His name. In the court of law, you swear on the Bible to "tell the truth, the whole truth and nothing but the truth, so help you, GOD". Yet many do not tell the truth when their confession is heard. GOD is a God of truth and associating His name with a lie is bringing dishonor to His name.

> *"Again, you have heard that it was said to those of old, 'You shall not swear falsely, but shall perform your oaths to the LORD.' But I say to you, do not swear at all: neither by heaven, for it is God's throne; nor by the earth, for it is His footstool; nor by Jerusalem, for it is the city of the great King. Nor shall you swear by your head, because you cannot make one hair white or black. But let your 'Yes' be 'Yes' and your 'No,' 'No.' For whatever is more than these is from the evil one. "*
>
> *- Matthew 5:33-37*

GOD's name is powerful. The name of JESUS is powerful. Demons tremble and flee at His name and people are healed by the name of JESUS. That is why the enemy loves to see GOD's people break this commandment. The demons know who has the authority and who does not. When you use GOD's name, or the name of JESUS haphazardly throughout the day, don't expect to see GOD's power and authority come over you when you pray.

Is this biblical?

> *Then some of the itinerant Jewish exorcists took it upon themselves to call the name of the Lord Jesus over those who had evil spirits, saying, "We exorcise you by the Jesus whom Paul preaches." Also, there were seven sons of Sceva, a Jewish chief priest, who did so. And the evil spirit answered and said, "Jesus I know, and Paul I know; but who are you?" Then the man in whom the evil spirit was leaped on them, overpowered them and prevailed against them so that they fled out of that house naked and wounded.*
>
> *- Acts 19:13-16*

JESUS said that if you ask anything in His name, He will do it. If you want to see your prayers answered, stop using the name of Jesus in a worthless, futile way. Give Him the glory, honor, and reverence that He deserves, and watch His authority and power come over you as you pray.

If you ask most people if they are a Christian, they will respond yes, yet their lifestyle is far from it. To be a Christian is to be Christ-like. You cannot call yourself a Christian or God's people and then do things that are going to bring dishonor or shame to His name. If you profess to be a Christian but live a life of lawlessness, you are taking His name in vain.

> *"Not everyone who says to Me, 'Lord, Lord,' shall enter the kingdom of heaven, but he who does the will of My Father in heaven. Many will say to Me in that day, 'Lord, Lord, have we not prophesied in Your name, cast out demons in Your name, and done many wonders in Your name? And then I will declare to them, I never knew you; depart from Me, you who practice lawlessness!"*
>
> *- Matthew 7:21-23*

It is time for God's people to give Him the honor and glory He deserves. His name is holy, treat it with respect. As Christians, we sometimes forget that we are God's witnesses not only with the words we speak but more importantly with our actions and the way we live our lives. If you are going to bear witness to Jesus's name, your lifestyle needs to reflect His character. There are so many blessings that come when people see the character of Jesus in your walk and your talk. People will notice!

Questions for Thought
1. What does it mean to take God's name in vain?
2. Why does God feel so strongly about His name?
3. What is lawlessness?

Break free from all the subtle ways you use God's name in vain. Refer to Section 3, Third Commandment to continue your process of deliverance.

Chapter 11

HAVE YOU TAKEN YOUR BREAK?

Commandment Four
"Remember the Sabbath day, to keep it holy. Six days you
shall labor and do all your work, but the seventh day is the
Sabbath of the LORD your God. In it, you shall do no work:
you, nor your son, nor your daughter, nor your male
servant, nor your female servant, nor your cattle, nor your
stranger who is within your gates. For in six days the LORD
made the heavens and the earth, the sea, and all that is in
them and rested the seventh day. Therefore, the LORD
blessed the Sabbath day and hallowed it."
- Exodus 20:8-11

This is the fourth and last of the commandments that specifically helps to define our proper relationship with GOD. The Hebrew word for Sabbath is Shabbat which means intermission.[1] Intermission from what? With today's fast-paced world, you need a break from your compulsive working lifestyle and take time to reflect on the goodness of GOD. He commands us to keep the Sabbath holy. For what purpose? It is time to cease from your daily routine and dedicate your time to Him. It is a time of rest and spiritual renewal. GOD wants you to have a personal relationship with Him, not a religion. You can strengthen your relationship with Him by celebrating Shabbat. Throughout the week you are so busy you don't take the proper time to rest and get into His presence. Shabbat is so important because it rejuvenates your body, mind, and spirit. GOD knew the

100

importance of the Sabbath, He established it since the beginning of time.

> *Thus, the heavens and the earth, and all the host of them, were finished. And on the seventh day, God ended His work which He had done, and He rested on the seventh day from all His work which He had done.*
>
> *- Genesis 2:1-2*

Why is the rest important?

GOD rested and the Sabbath was instituted. GOD did not need to rest, He is omnipotent. His creativity could have ended on the sixth day, but it did not. On the seventh day, He rested thus creating the Sabbath. He blessed it and made it holy. I'm sure during His time of rest GOD reflected on the past week and the creation He had made. He had just finished creating man on the sixth day and now wanted to spend time with His creation. The Sabbath is a time to draw close to GOD, thanking Him for the past week and asking for strength and wisdom for the week to come. You need times of rest to reflect on the goodness and mercies of GOD.

This commandment is a call to remember what GOD has done for you. It is a time to realize your physical, emotional, and spiritual well-being is dependent completely upon Him and your relationship with JESUS. He alone is your Savior, Deliverer, Healer, Sanctifier, and your Provider. If you constantly go, go, go, and do not take the time to rest, it will open the door to anxiety, frustration, fear, mental burnout, physical exhaustion, and spiritual emptiness. Could it be that the distance you feel between you and GOD is because you are not celebrating your Shabbat?

What are your actions saying to GOD?

I believe this is the most frequently broken commandment among Christians today. It is one of the hardest and most resisted of the commandments to follow because people misunderstand it and do not see it as a sin if they do not follow it. Did you know that honoring the Sabbath is a testing of your heart?

> *'I am the* LORD *your God; walk in My statutes, keep My judgments, and do them; hallow My Sabbaths, and they will be a sign between Me and you, that you may know that I am the* LORD *your God.'*
>
> *- Ezekiel 20:19-20*

The Sabbath is GOD's gift to you. It is not for GOD's benefit. It is to benefit you! No one can continue to break the Sabbath and keep his or her physical and mental health. Eventually one or the other, or even both will start to deteriorate.

For years I never honored the Sabbath because I didn't see it as a sin if I didn't. Because of working full time throughout the week, I would pack my Saturdays with all sorts of activities: cleaning, laundry, shopping, washing the car, etc. I was a perpetual doer. Relaxing was not in my vocabulary. Even when I tried to sit still, my mind was constantly going. I could not shut it off for even a minute. I would go to bed at night and it took forever to fall asleep. I would sleep but feel just as tired when I woke up.

My mind was in overload with thoughts and it eventually caught up with me. I was physically, mentally, and spiritually burned out. One Sunday service I was given a prophetic word that GOD was requiring 21 Shabbats or sickness and death were coming to visit me. This was a strong word and I took it before my LORD in prayer. In faith, I heeded the word and separated myself with GOD for the next 21 Saturdays. At first, it was very difficult because I kept thinking of all the things I needed to get done. But after several Shabbats, I was able to relax and concentrate while reading the Word and focus on Him. They say that it takes 21 days to break a habit. Busyness can be a terrible habit when you can't get it under control. It took 21 Shabbats to deliver me from my busyness. I now realize why GOD demanded 21 Shabbats. Through my obedience, I discovered the reality of two promises from GOD's Word.

- *"Come to Me all you who labor and are heavy laden, and I will give you rest."*

  - Matthew 11:28

- *But those who wait on the LORD shall renew their strength; they shall mount up with wings like eagles, they shall run and not be weary, they shall walk and not faint.*

  - Isaiah 40:31

Rest and strength come from GOD. You may try to get them through pills or an orthopedic mattress. These are just temporary fixes and will only cover up the root of your problem. Only GOD can put your mind at peace and give you the rest you need. Give all your cares to the LORD and rest in His presence. He will give you strength for each new day. I have found that when I am well-rested, I can think more clearly, and it is easier for me to hear the voice of GOD. I am so thankful to the LORD I obeyed the prophetic word. I now look forward to my Shabbats.

What are the extremes?

There are two extremes when looking at this commandment. The extreme to the left is to believe that you do not have to separate a day for GOD. Is lying, stealing, adultery, or murder a sin? Of course, they are. How then, can some of the Ten Commandments be considered a sin, yet this one not? These commandments were written in stone, and now should be written on your heart. Observing the Sabbath is a command from GOD, not an option. Don't lose out on the blessing of celebrating Shabbat.

The other extreme is to see anything you do other than resting in the presence of GOD on the Sabbath as a sin. Thinking in this way is very legalistic and this is exactly what the Pharisees tried to accuse JESUS of time and time again.

> *Now it happened, as He went into the house of one of the rulers of the Pharisees to eat bread on the Sabbath, that they watched Him closely. And behold, there was a certain man before Him who had dropsy. And Jesus, answering, spoke to the lawyers and Pharisees, saying, "Is it lawful to heal on the Sabbath?" But they kept silent. And He took him and healed him and let him go. Then He answered them saying, "Which of you, having a donkey or an ox that has fallen into a pit, will not immediately pull him out on the Sabbath day?" And they could not answer Him regarding these things.*
>
> *- Luke 14:1-6*

What is the purpose of the Sabbath?

By healing the man JESUS demonstrated that mercy and love prevailed and there was nothing wrong with doing good works for the LORD on the Sabbath. We read throughout the Gospels that many were healed and delivered on the Sabbath. In Mark 2 JESUS stated,

> *"The Sabbath was made for man, and not man for the Sabbath. Therefore, the Son of Man is also Lord of the Sabbath."*.
>
> *– Mark 2:27-28*

The Sabbath was made to be a blessing and not a set of legalistic rules that the Pharisees had turned it into. JESUS had authority over the Sabbath and performed many miracles on that day, setting individuals free from sickness and demonic strongholds. Follow His example. The purpose of the Sabbath is to draw people closer to GOD. When you reach out to those in need with mercy, compassion, and love, you are operating in the

Spirit of the Law. The heart of GOD always moves with compassion toward those who cry out to Him.

What if my job requires me to work?

According to the Hebrew calendar, the Sabbath begins at sunset Friday evening and ends at sunset Saturday evening. You may be saying to yourself, "But what if I can't get Saturdays off?" You may be like many others whose job requires you to work on Saturdays. You cannot be legalistic and say that you are sinning. It is a matter of the heart. If you separate one day for rest and seek the LORD, you are celebrating your Shabbat. The LORD knows your heart, and if you are diligently seeking Him, you will find Him. In the meantime, pray and ask the LORD to rearrange your schedule so you would not have to work on His Shabbat. However, if you chose to work on Saturday just to get some overtime and extra money, you are breaking the Sabbath and allowing the spirit of mammon to steal your blessing and intimacy with GOD.

How is your work ethics?

There is another part of this commandment that we must obey. This commandment states that we are to rest **after** six days of labor. GOD commands you to work. You are not to be idle. How is your work ethics? Are you giving 100% when you are at work? Does your work ethics reflect the character of JESUS? Without noticing, the people around you are watching to see if your actions line up with your testimony. Are you able to hold a steady job? Do you complain a lot about your work?

Are you a young adult living at home with little desire to find a job? If you are, you are taking advantage of and living at the expense of your parents. If you are out of school, you should be working and helping to pay for the living expenses or living on your own supporting yourself. You are not to be lazy at the expense of others.

Laziness casts one into a deep sleep, and an idle person will suffer hunger. He who keeps the commandment keeps his soul, but he who is careless of his ways will die.
- Proverbs 19:15-16

Many people want a paycheck but do not want to work for it. If they work, some give only 50% effort and lazily perform their job. Others rely on the welfare system to make ends meet. Although the welfare system was meant to be a blessing to the poor, it has become an avenue against work ethics. For some people, when they are given subsidized living arrangements, food stamps, and health care, they find it easier to stay on the system rather than going out to work. They would rather become lazy and this is contrary to the Word of GOD.

If anyone will not work, neither shall he eat.
- 2 Thessalonians 3:10

Good work ethics brings honor to the LORD and working six days a week opens the door to enjoy our well-earned Shabbat. You will enjoy the many blessings GOD has for your life. The Sabbath is your time to fellowship with Him. Build and strengthen your relationship with Him. Allow the LORD to use you to minister to those in need and further His kingdom. Reflect on GOD's goodness and how He has delivered you from the bondage of sin. If you are going to reach GOD's divine purpose for your life, obey the fourth commandment and rest as He has commanded.

Questions for Thought
1. How is celebrating the Sabbath a sign between you and GOD? (Exodus 20:19-20)
2. How can we become legalistic with celebrating the Sabbath?
3. What are the benefits of celebrating the Sabbath?
4. Why is laziness a sin?

Have You Taken Your Break?

Remove every hindrance that keeps you from resting as GOD commands you to do. Refer to Section 3, Fourth Commandment to continue your process of deliverance.

Chapter 12
HOW CAN I WITH SO MUCH PAIN?

Commandment Five
"Honor your father and your mother, that your days may be
long upon the land which the LORD *your God is giving you."*
- Exodus 20:12

Family is the fundamental component of the church and the basic building block of a nation. Honor your father and your mother is a commandment that calls attention to the family structure. The enemy knows the importance of the family, that is why Satan strives to destroy the family unit and bring so much pain and suffering. GOD intended the relationship between parents and their children to be positive, nurturing, and wholesome. However, we live in a fallen world full of imperfect people where sin abounds. Through their struggles with sin, parents end up doing and/or saying harmful things to their children and grandchildren. These actions often leave deep wounds in the lives of their children and could affect them for the rest of their lives.

It is very easy to love and honor someone when they treat you right and when they treat you with respect. But what if you were a victim of abuse, incest, or your father abandoned you when you were small? Are you expected to love and honor the one who brought so much pain into your life? I understand all too well this reality. It is something I grew up with and with the help of the HOLY SPIRIT I was able to overcome.

108

As a child, I was a victim of incest. I felt so ashamed, dirty, and abused as my grandfather molested me. My innocence was stolen from me at a very early age. I hated my grandfather for what he did to me. Growing up I never shared this with anyone because I was afraid no one would believe me, and I felt too ashamed to expose the truth. As time passed by, I began to have resentment towards my mother because it was her father that was molesting me. The abuse continued until I was older and strong enough to push my grandfather away. To bury my pain, I focused on making good grades and doing well in sports. My grandfather died during my high school years and I was relieved. I no longer had to see his face again, so I thought.

In my late teens and early adulthood, I began having dreams about my grandfather. What I thought was buried deep within had come to the surface. I struggled with depression most of my life and while in college I tried to commit suicide. The shame and guilt were too much for me to handle. God spared my life and I was placed on antidepressants. This just put a Band-Aid over my wounds, it didn't get to the root of the depression, nor did I receive the emotional healing I needed.

I was able to graduate and began working at a local hospital. One of my coworkers was a Christian and through her testimony and example of love, I started going to her church. It was almost a year of attending the church before I gave my life to the Lord. I will never forget that day. As I cried out to the Lord, I saw the word forgiveness in front of me. I knew God had forgiven me of all my sins as I accepted Jesus into my life. Holy Spirit began to tug at my heart, "Forgive your grandfather." I tried to reason with God, "But he hurt me so much." God responded, "I will heal your pain." Holy Spirit brought such conviction. I knew if I wanted God to forgive me of my sins, I had to forgive my grandfather.

I made a choice that day to forgive my grandfather and unleash all the resentment. There was so much healing that took place. Through a process of deliverance, I was able to let go of all the shame, guilt, and hatred I had towards myself. It felt so good to finally be set free. My testimony is proof that there is power in forgiveness. It didn't matter to my grandfather if I forgave him or not, he was already dead. But it made a big difference in my life and the freedom I received because of my obedience.

I was able to share about the abuse with my mother and asked forgiveness for the resentment I had towards her. What the enemy meant for evil, the LORD turned it around for His glory. Because of the healing GOD brought to my life, I have ministered to women who were victims of rape, incest, and abuse. I thank the LORD for his mercy over my life and how He uses me to bring hope to those who are suffering.

Maybe your pain is because your father abandoned you, or you were emotionally abused as a child. The pain may be so deep that you feel you can never forgive your parent, grandparent, stepfather, or whoever else represents a mother or father figure in your life. First, I want you to know that you are not alone. Many like yourself are going through the same pain that you are. Secondly, without JESUS in your life and the help of HOLY SPIRIT, you won't be able to forgive. It is only through His power and His strength that you can forgive someone who has brought such heartache. JESUS is the only one who can give you unconditional love for that person and bring healing to your soul. Forgiving is not saying that the individual didn't do anything wrong. Forgiveness helps you to keep your heart pure and bring the healing you need. If your mind is made up that you don't want to forgive the person, meditate on this scripture.

> *"For if you forgive men their trespasses, your heavenly Father will also forgive you. But if you do not forgive men their trespasses, neither will your Father forgive your trespasses."*
>
> *- Matthew 6:14-15*

Forgiveness isn't for the benefit of the person who wronged you. You are the one who benefits! When you harbor anger, resentment, unforgiveness, or bitterness in your heart, it only brings turmoil to your life. You end up feeling miserable and all those ill feelings lead to physical and/or emotional ailments which can lead to premature death. Ephesians 6 reminds us that the fifth commandment has a promise for our lives. Don't lose your blessings because of your unwillingness to forgive.

> *"Honor your father and mother", which is the first commandment with promise: "that it may be well with you and you may live long on the earth."*
> *- Ephesians 6:2-3*

When you hold onto bitterness and resentment, your focus is on the person who offended you. You are wasting most of your energy holding onto those destructive emotions. If you don't let go of them, they will eventually bring harm you to physically, emotionally, and/or spiritually.

> *Beloved, I pray that you may prosper in all things and be in health, just as your soul prospers.*
> *- 3 John 1: 2*

Refusal to forgive causes a lack of sleep, depression, chemical imbalance, and a weakened immune system. Research shows that almost every system in the body can be influenced by chronic stress. Those stressors include pent-up anger, guilt, and resentment. When chronic stress goes unreleased, it suppresses the body's immune system and ultimately manifests as illness. Emotional stress is a major contributing factor to the six leading causes of death in the United States.[1] If you continue to embrace those negative feelings, you are only hurting yourself.

How can I forgive my adulterous father?

Forgiveness is a choice only you can make. No one can make it for you. My ability to forgive my grandfather came easily.

111

However, for others that may not be the case. Sometimes it is a process and it takes time, as in the case of Sophia. She struggled with hatred towards her father for many years for committing adultery.

"I can remember since I was a little girl how my father was very unfaithful to my mother. Sometimes it was a relationship with one lady, other times he had several women at a time. Women would call our house and tell my mother that her husband was unfaithful and having an affair with them. My mother was very hurt, but she never divorced him. Because of her pain, she would always talk bad about my father and constantly remind me of his unfaithfulness and what a cheat he was. Hearing these words and seeing the pain my mother was suffering opened a door of resentment and a lack of forgiveness in my heart.

If my father did something wrong, my mother would send me to confront him. I was the mean person in the house that always confronted him. I remember when I was very young confronting him in the presence of one of the ladies he was dating. Once I even slapped him, pushed him, and knocked him down to the ground. This behavior demonstrated just how much hatred I had towards him. This continued throughout my life. I was a very sad, bitter individual, full of anger. I became very aggressive and constantly fought with my brother, sister, and cousins.

Time passed, I got married and because I never dealt with the anger, bitterness, and lack of forgiveness towards my father, these emotions began to manifest in my marriage. I began to have episodes of rage, screaming, and throwing dishes at my husband. My anger was uncontrollable. My husband was a GOD -fearing man and treated me with respect. I would get very upset over little things and would become very aggressive, even hit him at times. Everything from my past was manifesting, even though there was no reason for it.

When I began my walk with the LORD I learned about deliverance and realized I needed to go through this process to be free from my past. I was ministered to in the area of hatred and was able to forgive my father. For the vicious cycle of hatred and resentment to stop, I had to renounce vows of never forgiving my father or husband for certain things they had done to me. This was a key part of my deliverance. After this, I began to feel much better and my relationship with my husband grew stronger with each new day. However, I did not feel completely healed. I was given a word by one of the prophets of the church that I needed to go and ask forgiveness to my father for the way I treated him. My first reaction was, "Oh no, that is too much for me to ask for forgiveness from my dad. He will think he never did anything wrong. But I knew I needed to obey GOD's instructions.

During a family visit, I arranged to meet with my father privately. I went to his apartment, not knowing how he would respond but trusted in the LORD as I obeyed His instructions. "Dad, I need to ask your forgiveness because I was a bad daughter. I raised my hand against you, I should have never done that, I was aggressive and mean towards you." As I was asking forgiveness my father interrupted me and said, "No, No, quiet! Don't say that." My father began crying and said, "The one who needs to ask forgiveness is me." He began to recall everything that he had done wrong to us. He mentioned how much he missed my mom ever since she had passed away. He realizes the godly woman she was and now is suffering the consequences of loneliness. He began to ask for forgiveness for all his mistakes. This was a miraculous work of the LORD, knowing how proud my dad was. It was a beautiful time of reconciliation.

The reconciliation opened a door to a beautiful relationship with my father and me. Not only that, but it also opened his heart to accept JESUS as his personal Savior and he prayed the prayer of salvation. It was a time of complete healing and deliverance for my life and his. My father and I now have a beautiful relationship. When he comes to the states he always stays in my home and comes to church with my husband and me. At home, he connects via the Internet and hears the messages of ABBA Ministries every week. My marriage has been a beautiful work of the LORD. My struggles in my marriage all centered on the root of a lack of forgiveness towards my father. The LORD is good and has brought total healing and deliverance not only with my father but also with my relationship with my husband."

Through Sophia's willingness to forgive, not only was she healed and her relationship with her father restored, it softened the heart of her father and he was open to receive the love of JESUS. Forgiveness is a powerful tool you can use to change the lives of others.

Why did my parents give me up?

It's hard to understand why a mother would give up her infant child. Some do so because they are too young or unfit to take care of the child. Others do so to give the child a better life. But what if your parents gave you up when you were very young but kept your siblings. Could you imagine the rejection that could be felt! This is what Jacob faced growing up.

"A few months after I was born my parents gave me to my grandparents to raise me. My grandparents cared for me as if I were their son. Outwardly it appeared I was very happy because I was being well cared for. However, this was not the case. As I grew older, a root of bitterness began to form in my heart. I could not understand why my parents gave me up yet kept and raised my two younger brothers. I would visit my parents from time to time but could not feel their love. I felt very rejected because of their lack of affection towards me and began to have resentment and hatred towards them.

How Can I With So Much Pain?

As time passed, I began to detest my brothers. I kept wondering what it was about me that my parents did not like. I saw how much they cared for my brothers and how they always did things together as a family should. My brothers had a lighter skin tone and green eyes, I had dark skin and brown eyes. I wondered if this was the reason for them not accepting me as their son.

One weekend I went to stay with my parents and brothers. That night my father came home very drunk and started beating my mother and split her head open. I swore that when I got older, I would kill him, and I ran back to my grandparent's house. I will never forget that day and the effect it had on me. The resentment and hatred I had towards him intensified even more.

Shortly after this incident, my father was killed. I was relieved yet I felt like every part of me was shaken. I realized that a part of me still loved my father, despite the pain of the rejection that was there. I moved from my grandparents' house to live with my mom and two younger brothers. However, there was constant fighting because of the root of hatred and rejection that was still in my heart. I continued to disrespect my mother. A year later my mom remarried and abandoned me and my two brothers. I was only twelve years old at the time. I was forced to go to work so I could provide for my brothers. My heart was filled with hate toward my mother. My brothers were full of hatred towards her as well. The devil had such a grip on my heart that one day in front of my brothers and relatives I screamed that my mother was my shame and that she was the worst thing that ever happened to me. What a great dishonor I made towards my mother. I was miserable inside and without faith and hope.

One of my aunts reached out to me and invited me to church. I started to attend and a month later I accepted the LORD as my Savior. Two years later I went on a retreat and they spoke about lack of forgiveness. During the retreat, I had a deep encounter with the LORD. HOLY SPIRIT. HOLY SPIRIT brought such conviction of my sins. The resentment towards my mother and brothers that was buried in my heart was the quickest way to take me to

115

hell. It was at this moment that I understood the significance of forgiving my mother and brothers and the revelation of the importance of honoring my mother.

Through my process of healing the LORD was softening my heart and revealing His love for me. In my intimacy with the LORD, I asked Him why my mother did not give me love. The answer I received was simple. He told me that no one can give what they never received. It was at that moment I realized my mother never felt loved. That truth tugged at my heart. I could not beg my mother for love and expect it because she never received love.

Because I had received the love of GOD, I knew I had to reciprocate that love. I took the first step in showing love to my mother. I asked her for forgiveness for the resentment and hatred I had towards her and for dishonoring her. I understood that there is a purpose of GOD for my life. He broke the chains of lack of forgiveness, resentment, and rejection from my life. Now I can call my mom and brothers and tell them that I love them.

The LORD opened my heart to fall in love again. I am happily married and have two beautiful daughters. I now understand how the enemy wanted to destroy my life and rob me of my destiny. Just breaking one commandment of the LORD leaves the door wide open for the enemy to bring havoc to your life. I thank the LORD for His mercy over my life."

You won't be able to understand the behavior of others unless you know what that individual has gone through. Ask the LORD to show you why your mother or father treated you the way they did. Just like in Jacob's case, the LORD will show you the root of their behavior. You just need to seek Him with an open heart and ask Him for the answers you are searching for.

Is it possible to honor an alcoholic father?

It is not easy living with a parent who is an alcoholic. An alcoholic can destroy the family and cause harmful effects that can last a lifetime. Sadly, while under the influence of alcohol, a parent can say or do things that are totally out of their control. Their behavior can be very devastating. Lives can be destroyed. Unfortunately, alcoholics cannot see the damage they are causing to the family, nor do they care. This was the life of Nancy.

"It is not always easy to follow this instruction from the LORD, but when we do the LORD is very pleased with us. Exodus 20:12 commands us to honor our father and mother. That's easy to do when you have loving parents who treat you right. I grew up in a very bad home environment and obeying this commandment seemed impossible for me to do. My father was an alcoholic, heavily drinking most of the time. In his drunken state, he was constantly abusive toward me, my brother, my sister, and my mother. His abuse was mostly verbal, but at times it became physical. As I got older, his drinking got worse and so did his abuse. Once he woke me up at three o'clock in the morning, screaming at the top of his lungs, and telling me I was worth nothing and hated the day I was born. He blamed me for every problem he had in his life.

Once I turned eighteen, I left the house and did not return for a year. However, HOLY SPIRIT began to bring conviction to my heart. He reminded me of Exodus 20:12 where I was to honor my father. I asked the LORD, "How am I supposed to honor the man that has brought such destruction to my life?" He led me to Ephesians 6:12 which states the following:

"For we do not wrestle against flesh and blood, but against principalities, against powers, against the rulers of darkness of this age, against spiritual hosts of wickedness in the heavenly places."
- Ephesians 6:12

I knew I had to forgive my dad and it was a choice I decided to take. It was not easy to rebuild a relationship with him, but the LORD was faithful and helped me through the process. I kept praying for his salvation and GOD was faithful to answer my prayers. My dad dedicated himself to the LORD, gave up drinking, and started going back to church. A few years later my father died because of the effects the alcohol had on his body. I thank the LORD that I was able to restore my relationship with him before GOD took him home. The LORD is faithful when we are obedient to his instructions."

Nancy was able to rebuild her relationship with her father before his death. Many individuals are not as fortunate, and it leaves a deep hole in their soul and opens the door for the enemy to bring guilt and accusation. Don't give him that opportunity. Ask the LORD to bring healing to your family relationships.

My father abandoned me, and my mother abused me, how can I forgive?

Some children grow up without a father because the individual chooses not to take on the responsibility of fatherhood. Some children are raised by two parents but in an environment of physical and/or emotional abuse. Think of the difficulty of being raised in a home where your father abandoned you and your mother was very abusive. This was the case with Kassandra. Despite all this, as a teenager, she asked JESUS into her life and allowed the LORD to bring the healing and deliverance she needed.

"I had a very difficult childhood. My family was attacked by the enemy and we suffered greatly. I was eight years of age when my father left us. My mother was 28 years old and was left all by herself to raise five children. She was devastated and with many problems. She was very cold towards my sisters and me and did

118

not realize how abusive her behavior was. While growing up I did not feel her love and always felt that there was something wrong with me. With time, I began to develop insecurities and fears. Hatred began to fill my heart because of how she mistreated me. My mom worked full time and that left me and my sisters responsible for the chores around the house. I had so much fear when I was around her. I didn't know if she was going to beat me, scream at me, or make me do some odd chores like washing dishes or cleaning gum that was stuck on the floor. One of her favorite corrections was to grab my arm and press her nails into me to the point of drawing blood. I was so afraid of her.

Throughout my adolescent years, I felt lonely and unloved. I was able to find the love that I was lacking from my mother through my aunt and the mothers of my friends. They always made me feel loved and wanted. At the age of fifteen my life changed, I accepted JESUS as my personal Savior, and I began to understand why my mother was so full of bitterness, sadness, and rage. But that did not rid my feelings of hatred and rejection towards her. My mother nor I could hold each other and feel a mother-daughter bond. I would try to avoid her whenever I could. My decision to follow JESUS caused my mother to manifest even more. My sisters would go to parties and come home late, and nothing would happen to them. But if I came home late from church, she would beat me and ground me or would not allow me to go to the youth group or Sunday services. I began to lie to attend church.

One of the worst moments I ever had with my mom was when I was around 18 years old. She had blamed me for something that I did not do, and her anger got out of control. She began to hit me, pull my hair, and bang my head against the walls. She scratched me and insulted me. She pushed me down the stairs, but I kept running away from her and managed to get inside my bedroom and lock the door. She knocked on the door and when I wouldn't open it, she left and in time calmed herself down. This was the worst night of my life. The next day I woke up with bruises all over my body and a huge pain in my heart. I was full of sadness and hatred at the same time. I left my house and stayed at a friend's house for about a month.

The LORD began to speak to me a lot during that month. He first spoke to me regarding my behavior and attitude as a daughter, showing me my faults and my sins. I was not honoring my mother as the commandment instructs me to do. HOLY SPIRIT brought conviction and I repented and ask forgiveness to the LORD for having hatred towards my mother and for lying to her. My mother's darkness needed the light of JESUS that was inside of me to shine upon her. The LORD began to show me how broken and hopeless my mother felt. Her aggressiveness was her way of coping with her pain and suffering. This did not justify her behavior, but I was able to understand why she was such an abusive mother.

As the LORD continued to work in my life, I knew I had to go and ask forgiveness from my mother for the things I did wrong. This was not going to be easy for me because I was never able to talk to my mother, nor share my feelings as a daughter should. The LORD gave me the strength and courage to sit down with her and express everything I was feeling inside. I asked for forgiveness and she accepted it. We cried and she asked me for forgiveness as well. How beautiful is the LORD! This was the beginning process for my mother. The LORD began to work little by little in her life until one day she accepted JESUS as her Savior. What a life-changing decision she made. I saw my mother change from a mean abusive mother to a beautiful woman of GOD. I can say with such joy that the promises of GOD's Word are a big AMEN. He never fails! The change was dramatic. GOD gave me a new mom and I cherish the intimate mother-daughter relationship we now experience. My LORD has healed me and restored me in such a mighty way. Isn't GOD beautiful!"

You may be a Christian teenager who is dealing with non-Christian parents. I hope the testimony of Kassandra helps you to see what an important role you have in sharing the light of JESUS to your parents. If you are struggling with obeying this commandment, I hope the above testimonies give you hope for your situation. Each testimony sheds light on the various ways the enemy tries to destroy families. Whether your situation reflects upon one of these testimonies or if your family crisis is different, all have one thing in common. They will lead you down a path of destruction through strongholds of hatred, resentment, bitterness, and lack of forgiveness if the LORD does not intervene in your life.

Is there an option?

Forgiveness is a powerful tool. It is what brought the healing and deliverance to the individuals of the testimonies you just read. They not only forgave, but they were also able to honor their parent, despite the wrong that was done to them. You may think that forgiving your father and/or your mother is impossible. All things are possible if you allow the LORD to help you. JESUS died on the cross for your sins and your pain. If you do not have a personal relationship with Him, ask Him to be LORD and Savior of your life. Nail your pain to the cross. Give it to JESUS and see the power of healing and restoration come to your life. No matter what your upbringing was like or if you are facing challenges now, nothing is too difficult for the LORD. Trust Him today for you healing and freedom.

You may be asking, "Why should I honor my father or my mother when I was treated in such a terrible way? I'll forgive them, but I'm not going to honor them. They don't deserve it." Honoring your father and mother is a command from GOD. It does not say to honor your father and your mother if they treat you right. This command is not optional, nor is it conditional. You are commanded to honor your father and mother no matter what! This must be applied to anyone who fulfills the role of a parent: biological parents, grandparents, in-laws, adoptive parents, stepparents, foster parents, and your spiritual parents. Honor your parents not because you think they deserve it, but because GOD requires it of you. The LORD will hold your parents accountable for the way they have raised you and mistreated you. You have a responsibility to honor them. No matter how difficult your childhood is or was, if you allow the LORD to intervene, He will bring healing to your life and give you the strength to forgive and honor them.

How do you see your Heavenly FATHER?

You may be an adult now but remember how your parents treated you as a child. Often the way you view and relate to your earthly father is how you view and relate to your Heavenly FATHER An individual who has been abused or abandoned by their father may not have a problem receiving JESUS as their personal Savior but may struggle with the fact that they have a Heavenly Father who deeply cares for them. Because of personal hurts and needs, some have a distorted view of who GOD is. How can you trust in a Heavenly Father you cannot see when growing up your earthly father was never around? This was the case with Jonathan. Read how the LORD ministered to his life.

"I was born in Puerto Rico and when I was two years old my family migrated to New York City. We moved into a furnished room in Brooklyn. I was the fifth of seven children and you can only imagine how cramped we were. My mother stayed home to tend to our needs as our father went to work. My father was a hardworking man. He often worked long hours to support his family. As time passed, my father was able to buy a multi-family house. This house was our new home. We seemed to be living the "American dream".

As I grew older, I noticed a change in my father and realized that my father was an abusive man. He was getting more and more aggressive, both physically and verbally, to my family. He would often take his frustrations and insecurities out on the family. We were very fearful of him because when he arrived home we wouldn't know when or where he would beat us. Many times, we received severe beatings over minor infractions of his rules and regulations. At the age of ten, my father abandoned us. My mother, brothers, sisters, and I went through very difficult times. We lost the apartment we were living in, didn't know what we were going to eat from one day to the next, nor where we were going to stay. My mother divided us, and we lived with aunts and uncles until she could get things in order. I missed five months of school because of the moving around and when I returned to school I not only had to catch up with what I had missed but also keep up with the new material being taught so I would not be held back at the end of the school year. All of this brought a lot of anger, resentment, and bitterness towards my father. To add salt to the wound, years later I found out my father only lived about two miles away. He lived so close to us but didn't care where we lived or how we were doing. He provided no financial support to my mother for raising us. From the time my father left until the day he died, I only saw him two or three times. During those visits, there was no father-son bond. I felt indifferent towards him and didn't care if I ever saw him again.

One night I was lying in bed and had a vision about my father. This was unusual for me since I hadn't thought about him for years. The LORD reminded me of a time that my father demonstrated his love and compassion towards me. I was around six years old. I was taken to the hospital to have the cast removed from both of my legs. I was born with club feet and this was a final step in the long and difficult process of straightening out my feet. From being in the casts for many months, my leg muscles were very weak, I felt unstable and was unable to walk. My father carried me in his arms out of the hospital and into the car and when we arrived home, he carried me to our second-floor apartment. I felt safe and secure as never before. I felt joy and happiness in knowing that I could depend on him.

The vision I just share was the only time in my life that I ever felt the love from my father. Why was the LORD bringing this memory to the surface? It was because GOD wanted to bring healing to my life. There was a void in my life, and I couldn't accept the love of a father from anyone, not even a pastor. The LORD began to show me that through all the hard times in my life, He was there. Through the desert times, He was there. He carried me when my legs were too weak to sustain me. When I was lost and couldn't find my way, He was there to direct my path. GOD was a Father that I could rely on. He would never leave me, nor forsake me. He would be my FATHER if I would only accept His Fatherhood. His love filled my room and I knew it was real. On that day I accepted the LORD's Fatherhood over my life. Through my tears and sobs, GOD was emotionally healing me. I could feel all the anger, resentment, and bitterness I had towards my real father leave me as I embraced the love of my Heavenly FATHER. The deep wounds of my childhood were being healed. That fragment of my soul that was trapped in a soul jail of abandonment was set free as I welcomed the love and adoption of my Heavenly FATHER. I will always be thankful to my LORD for His mercy and compassion in my life."

Don't let the lack of love or distorted love you received from your earthly father close your heart to the love of your Heavenly FATHER. Just like Jonathan, your Heavenly FATHER is waiting with open arms to receive you. Feel His embrace and allow Him to fill you with His love. Don't see Him as someone far away who can't be reached. Allow Him to enter your life in a personal way and begin a new relationship with ABBA, FATHER.

What does it mean to honor?

What does it mean to honor our parents? The original Hebrew word from Exodus 20 is *kabed* which means "to make weighty or to give weight to"[2]. If you look at the definition from the Greek used in Matthew 19:19 where JESUS is talking about GOD's commandments to the rich young ruler, honor means to revere or to value[3]. To honor your father and mother means to value them. For a person to carry a lot of weight implies the individual is of great importance and should be treated with respect. To honor is to give an individual their rightful place. It was your parents who brought you into the world. They have a unique place in your life. Without them, you would have never been born. They may not have done a good job. Maybe they were abused as a child and that is the only way they know how to act. This does not excuse their behavior, but for some, it is their reality.

If you are under the age of eighteen and your parents or someone else is abusing you, GOD does not want you to live under such oppression. Fear or shame may be stopping you from getting help. Don't keep this hidden. Honoring your parents does not mean you have to take their abuse. Tell a relative, a teacher, your youth pastor, or a guidance counselor. Tell someone so you don't have to face this on your own and you and your parents can receive the help that is needed.

How do we show honor?

When you have a personal relationship with your Heavenly FATHER, you honor Him through your obedience. You honor Him because He created you and saved you from eternal judgment. Just as you honor Him, you must honor those who GOD chose to bring you into this world. You honor your father and mother simply because they are your parents. Just as we honor GOD through obedience, we honor our earthly parents through obedience as well. JESUS set the example Himself by honoring His earthly parents.

> *Then He went down with them and came to Nazareth and was subject to them, but His mother kept all things in her heart. And Jesus increased in wisdom and stature, and in favor with God and men.*
>
> *- Luke 2:51-52*

JESUS was subject to His parents. What does that mean? The original Greek root for the word subject is *hupotasso* which means to be under obedience or to submit yourself.[4] JESUS obeyed his parents and submitted to their authority. JESUS also obeyed GOD's commandments (John 15:10) and submitted Himself to the will of His Heavenly FATHER.

"O My Father, if it is possible, let this cup pass from Me; nevertheless, not as I will, but as You will."

- Matthew 26:39

Children obey your parents in all things; for this is well-pleasing to the Lord.

- Colossians 3:20

If your parents are not asking you to do something contrary to the Word of GOD, you need to obey them. You may not always agree with what they are asking or telling you to do, but it is the right thing to do. They are trying to protect you and looking out for your best interest. Many times, they are trying to stop you from making the same mistakes in life that they made. Obedience pleases the heart of GOD and it will bring blessings to your life. When you grow older you will realize your parents gave you wise counsel.

How do you respond?

You honor your parents through your actions and your words. To a small child, honor means to obey. To an adolescent, it is much more than just obeying. It is affirming their dignity and worth. You may not understand why parents ask you to do certain things or prohibit you from doing what you want to do. In most cases, they are looking after your best interest. Your actions and words will speak volumes regarding what is really in your heart.

What is your attitude when your parents give you instructions that you don't agree with? Do you look down on them with hatred? Do you obey with a grudge in your heart? Maybe you are one who gets angry and talks back to your father and/or mother. What thoughts do you whisper to yourself when you are disciplined? Do you mimic or mock their actions? How do you address your father or mother? Do you refer to them as an old man or an old lady? This is being very disrespectful. Parents should be addressed with names that bring honor, not disrespect.

Did you ask first?

Have you ever taken money from your parents without asking and never returned it? Often children do not see this as stealing. They grab money from their parent's wallets without asking, justifying themselves by thinking their parents would say yes if they asked. Your parent's property does not automatically become yours. Taking or borrowing without permission is stealing.

> *Whoever robs his father or his mother, and says, "It is no transgression," the same is companion to a destroyer.*
> *- Proverbs 28:24*

The Word of GOD associates someone who thinks there is nothing wrong with stealing from their parents with a destroyer. The original Hebrew word for a destroyer is *shachath* which means corrupter or spoiler in the original Hebrew text.[5] Teach your children while they are young that taking things from others without asking is a sin.

"Savanna shared with me a concern she and her husband had with one of her children. Over several months they noticed money missing from their wallets. Friends would come to visit and after leaving, discover money was taken from their purses. They set a trap and discovered it was the oldest daughter who was stealing. They confronted Molly with the Word of GOD, disciplined her, and told her if she continued, she would go to hell and if she tried this outside the house she could potentially go to jail. HOLY SPIRIT brought the needed conviction. She asked forgiveness and did not steal again. To restore her parents, Molly continued to do her chores, but without an allowance for a month. She learned a valuable lesson."

Meditate on the following scriptures and ask the Lord to bring to remembrance any time you have dishonored your mother or father.

A fool despises his father's instruction, but he who receives correction is prudent.
- Proverbs 15:5

"He who mistreats his father and chases away his mother is a son who causes shame and brings reproach."
- Proverbs 19:26

There is a generation that curses its father and does not bless its mother. There is a generation whose teeth are like swords, and whose fangs are like knives.
- Proverbs 30: 11, 14

The eye that mocks his father, and scorns obedience to his mother, the ravens of the valley will pick it out, and the young eagles will eat it.
- Proverbs 30:17

And he who strikes his father, or his mother shall surely be put to death.
- Exodus 21:15

When does honoring our parents cease?

Honoring our parents does not cease when we become adults. It is a lifetime commitment until the Lord takes them home to be with Him. As parents get older, they may need to be physically cared for. Some exploit their parents financially because they feel it is owed to them after caring for their aging parents. They prey upon their parents without them even being aware of it. According to research funded by the U.S. Justice Department, about 1 in 10 Americans aged 60+ have experienced some form of elderly abuse, in 60% of the cases the perpetrator is a family member.[6] Being at a disadvantage, either physically or mentally, does not give you a right to take advantage of your parent's declining health. I have heard of a sibling fighting with another sibling over their parent's money, thinking it is theirs even though their mother or father is still alive. This is so disrespectful, and GOD sees it as sin.

Sometimes parents may need financial support as well. You may need to assist them in providing the proper nutrition or assist financially for a caregiver to take care of them while you work. Failing to fulfill a caretaking obligation is neglect and is considered a felony. You would think that family members would provide the best of care, but often this is not the case. Even though you have busy lives, it is your responsibility to make sure the needs of your parents are met. Everyone wants to feel loved and wanted. That does not change when you grow older. When was the last time you have called your mother or father to see how they were doing or to tell them you loved them? Many elderlies are placed in nursing homes because their adult children ignore their responsibility. It's not that they can't take care of them, but they choose not to because of the inconvenience. Once placed in the home they rarely visit and rarely call. It is one thing to place a loved one in a nursing home so they can receive the medical care that they need. But to place them there because you find them a burden is selfish and inexcusable.

> *Honor widows who are really widows. But if any widow has children or grandchildren, let them first learn to show piety at home and to repay their parents; for this is good and acceptable before God. But if anyone does not provide for his own, and especially for those of his household, he has denied the faith and is worse than an unbeliever.*
>
> *- 1 Timothy 5:3-4, 8*

Honor and respect for parents begin at home. As a believer, you have an obligation before the LORD to tend to the needs of your family. When a Christian does not care for their elderly as they should, it does not leave a good testimony for nonbelievers. You are denying the faith and your testimony is in vain when you neglect the needs of your family. JESUS confronted the Pharisees with their ritual acts yet ignoring the Word of GOD.

> *"But you say, 'If a man says to his father or mother, "Whatever profit you might have received from me is Corban"* — *' (that is, a gift to God), then you no longer let him do anything for his father or his mother, making the Word of God of no effect through your tradition which you have handed down. And many such things you do."*
> — *Mark 7:11-13*

JESUS was condemning the Pharisees for their man-made traditions which cause individuals to break the commandments of GOD. A Corban was something dedicated and set apart for GOD's use. Once declared, it could not be revoked. The Pharisees encouraged people to make such gifts to the temple while neglecting their responsibility to care for their parents. JESUS was making a point that using the Corban as an excuse for refusing to help one's parents who are in need is a sin. They were placing their man-made law above one of GOD's Ten Commandments. You cannot give special offerings to the LORD and expect Him to bless them if you are neglecting the needs of your parents.

The LORD gave me the blessing and opportunity to care for my ninety-eight-year-old mother. She had dementia and at times it was very challenging, but through the help of HOLY SPIRIT, my husband and I were able to fulfill her wishes not to be placed in a nursing home. I give thanks to my LORD for the opportunity to honor my mother in this way.

Your upbringing does not have to define who you are today. Children, it is time to make amends and find the freedom you need so you can honor your parents. Allow the LORD to heal and restore relationships within your family. If your parents are no longer living, He wants to heal your soul so you can have a healthy relationship with your children. Parents, GOD wants to heal and restore your relationship with your children. Receive the healing He has for you and your family.

Questions for Thought
1. What promise is attached to honoring your parents?
2. What will happen if you cannot forgive your parents for how they raised you?
3. What does the Word say about children who do not care for their widow parents? (1 Timothy 5)

Refer to Section 3, Fifth Commandment to continue your process of deliverance.

Chapter 13

HOW IS YOUR ANGER?

Commandment Six
"You shall not kill."
- Exodus 20:13

Depending on which Bible translation you read, you will see the sixth commandment written as "You shall not kill" or "You shall not murder". The Hebrew root for the word kill is *ratsach*, which means to dash in pieces, to murder, or slay[1]. To kill and to murder are not the same, the motives behind each are different. There is an underlying root of hatred that motivates a person to commit murder. You can kill someone and not have any hatred in your heart. It's only when you commit murder that this commandment is violated. There are times that killing is justified. Let's look at the Word of GOD for examples.

When is killing not murder?

> *"Whoever sheds man's blood, by man his blood shall be shed".*
>
> *- Genesis 9:6*

According to the above scripture, GOD allows capital punishment. If you are selected for jury duty on a criminal case and the individual is found guilty of murder, you do not have to feel guilty selecting the death penalty as a punishment.

"If the thief is found breaking in, and he is struck so that he dies, there shall be no guilt for his bloodshed."

- Exodus 22:2

You have a biblical right to protect yourself if your life is in danger. According to the law, you also have a legal right to do so. There is a stand-your-ground law that states that a person can use self-defense when one believes their life is in danger, this includes deadly force. This law grants immunity to criminal charges and civil lawsuits.

"Take a census of all the congregation of the children of Israel, by their families, by their fathers; houses, according to the number of names, every male individually, from twenty years old and above-all who are able to go to war in Israel."

- Numbers 1:2-3

If the government calls for a mandatory enlistment into the army, you have a moral, legal, and biblical obligation to do so. If you go to war under the orders of the government, you have a right to protect your country. The enemy is good at placing guilt upon you. If you have killed someone because of one of these examples, do not let the enemy put guilt upon you. You had no criminal intent in your heart. Satan has no legal right to accuse you.

What is the difference?

A great example of explaining the difference between killing and murder is through the life of King David. GOD's hand of protection was over King David in many wars. GOD did not hold him accountable for killing thousands in a battle. However, when Uriah was killed in battle, GOD blamed King David for his death. Although he was not the one to strike Uriah dead, GOD saw the intent of David's heart.

"And he wrote in the letter, saying, "Set Uriah in the forefront of the hottest battle, and retreat from him, that he may be struck down and die."

- 2 Samuel 11:15

Then Nathan said to David, "You are the man! Thus says the LORD God of Israel: 'I anointed you king over Israel, and I delivered you from the hand of Saul. I gave you your master's house and your master's wives into your keeping and gave you the house of Israel and Judah. And if that had been too little, I also would have given you much more! Why have you despised the commandment of the LORD, to do evil in His sight? You have killed Uriah the Hittite with the sword; you have taken his wife to be your wife and have killed him with the sword of the people of Ammon.'"

- 2 Samuel 12:7-9

You don't have to be the one killing a person to be guilty of murder. If a person has another individual do the job, he/she is just as guilty of murder as the person who follows through with the crime. You can attempt to murder someone, and although the person survives, you will be charged with attempted manslaughter. In GOD's eyes, you have already committed murder, you intended to kill. King David had Uriah killed to cover up his sin. Because he lusted for Bathsheba, he not only broke this commandment, he also broke the seventh, eighth, and tenth commandments as well. Nothing is hidden from GOD. He had appointed King David to build His temple, but because his hands were stained with blood, that prophetic assignment was taken away from him. King David repented, but his sin cost him his son's life.

Have you ever bullied?

We are created in the image of GOD. (Genesis 1:26) When you abuse someone, whether physically, emotionally, sexually, or psychologically you are abusing the image of GOD in that person. All forms of abuse are unacceptable, and GOD detests them.

The LORD tests the righteous, but the wicked and the one who loves violence His soul hates.

- Psalm 11:5

Those who love violence, GOD hates. No one has the right to use their uncontrollable anger or jealousy to prey on an individual. Many times, victims are beaten so badly, they wish they were dead. Those trapped in a vicious cycle of abuse have lost all sense of dignity and are fearful of their life if they leave. Psychological and emotional abuse can kill a person's self-esteem and self-worth. Social bullying is a form of violence. The intent is to belittle and bring harm to an individual. Teenagers are usually the victims and they fall into depression and commit suicide because they can't handle the shame and humiliation. All this malice is senseless and is seen as a sin in the eyes of GOD.

When does life begin?

If you were to ask the question, "When does life begin?" you will receive various responses. Although there is much controversy about this question, you must follow GOD's Law, not the laws of the land. Even though abortion is legal in some countries, it does not make it right in the eyes of GOD. Abortion is murder and a violation of the sixth commandment. GOD's Word tells us that He knows us before we were formed in the womb.

Then the word of the LORD came to me, saying; "Before I formed you in the womb, I knew you; before you were born, I sanctified you; I ordained you a prophet to the nations."

- Jeremiah 1:4-5

Where is the respect for life? Life is precious, yet many choose to throw it in the trash or have it used for scientific purposes. That is what happens to the life of a fetus after an abortion. When does life begin? It begins as soon as conception takes place! There is blood circulating in that developing tissue.

'For the life of the flesh is in the blood.'
- Leviticus 17:11

A fetus is not just a piece of flesh, it is life. By the fifth week after fertilization, the heart and circulatory system are already beginning to form. Many women are unaware they are pregnant yet, however, human cells are multiplying and developing body systems. Pro-choice advocates support their stand on abortion by stating women have a right to do what they want with their bodies. They believe they have a right to decide if they want to continue a pregnancy or terminate it. Their body is not their own, it belongs to GOD.

> *Or do you not know that your body is the temple of the Holy Spirit who is in you, whom you have from God, and you are not your own?*
> *- 1 Corinthians 6:19*

What about the rights of the unborn child? I know of individuals who have had an abortion and years later struggle with their decision. One friend tells me of how depressed she gets every year right around the time the baby would have been born. It is only when you find the mercy of the LORD and forgiveness of sin that you can be free. Abigail found that forgiveness.

"While in college I always stood up for pro-life, never thinking I would ever waiver from that belief. However, after graduating from college I became very rebellious and full of pride. I fell in love with a married man who was separated from his wife and became pregnant. Because his divorce was not final, he thought the easiest solution would be to have an abortion. I thought I knew what love was and agreed to have an abortion just to show him how much I loved him. As I continued in the relationship, I got pregnant again and had my second abortion.

My life took a downward spiral increasing the use of drugs and alcohol. I blamed GOD and allowed myself to believe that if he had sent me the right man into my life, this would never have happened. I lost my identity and self-respect. The relationship ended and I soon began another. After my third abortion, I knew my lifestyle could not continue and began a different path for my life. I buried my shame, married, and pursued a career in teaching. After the birth of my daughter, I returned to the church, wanting to set a good example and raise her in a Christian home.

Drugs and alcohol were no longer a part of my life. I appeared to be this perfect Christian, but no one knew the mask I was wearing regarding my past. I know GOD has forgiven me, but I was not ready to share my secret. My pastor challenged everyone in the church to write down their testimonies to share and encourage others. Without the testimony of GOD's goodness in my life, the enemy still had a hold of my soul. I needed to let go of my shame. I'm not proud of the abortions I have had, but I give glory to my LORD for the freedom I now have because of His mercy and love for me. If you are struggling with guilt or shame because of an abortion you have had, know that GOD wants to bring healing to your life too. Just call upon him, ask forgiveness, and allow Him to bring the deliverance you need to set you free."

America is under a curse for allowing the shedding of innocent blood with the passing of the Supreme Court ruling of Roe vs Wade, legalizing abortion. This has opened the door for a spirit of death to be over the land. That is why you see an increase in senseless murders and vehicular homicides. When Cain killed his brother Abel, the Word tells us that the voice of his brother's blood cried out to GOD (Genesis 4). Abortions do not go unnoticed by GOD and judgment will come if it hasn't already.

What about suicide?

Suicide rates among young people have continued to soar in recent years, especially among 15- to 19-year-olds.[2] I have had many people ask me if I thought people who commit suicide would go to hell. I believe it depends on a person's state of mind. If an individual is mentally ill or has a chemical imbalance and does not know what they are doing, I do not believe GOD will send them to hell. Only GOD knows a person's state of mind when they commit suicide. If you are suffering from depression and have suicidal thoughts, don't let Satan destroy your life. Don't allow him to make you think life is not worth living. Things may seem grim now, but better days are ahead. There is someone who loves you very much. His name is JESUS. Cry out to Him. He can bring hope to your situation. With the help of HOLY SPIRIT, you can find to strength to continue. GOD has a purpose and plan for your life. Read the testimony of Roxanne. She was tormented with depression but found the help she needed

"My downward spiral began when I started hanging out with the wrong people. Because of the bad influence, my grades dropped, I had boyfriend issues and became very depressed. A friend gave me advice and told me that she cuts herself sometimes and it helps her deal with the pain. At the time I thought she was my best friend, like my sister, but no sister tells you to cut yourself. I tried it for the first time and convinced myself that it took the pain away. Little did I know it just made everything worst. I got no sleep, I did no homework, during the days I would wear a fake smile, and during the nights I would cry and cry, then I would cut. I became suicidal and prayed and ask for help even though I didn't believe I could get an answer to my prayer. The cutting got out of control and I would cut my arms and both legs from ankle to thigh. It was an addiction, I couldn't stop. I ran out of space to cut and I would go over old cuts to make them deeper.

My real best friend also struggled with depression. We were both addicted to the pain of cutting and it got so twisted that we embraced and loved our depression, we were both suicidal and we considered that fun. Then I started dating someone and the depression lifted, but the desire to cut myself was still there. I was admitted to a mental facility and was under medical care for about four days. This was the first time my parents found out about my being depressed and cutting myself. When I was discharged from the hospital, I didn't cut for two weeks. I thought I was healed but I didn't know that I needed JESUS to be truly healed. I started cutting again and it got so much worse. Every time I saw my blood, I would smile but it wasn't normal, it was a demonic smile.

Around two months later my friend gave her life to JESUS and her life changed for the good. She invited me to go to church with her. Even though I was skeptical, I decided to go. I went and I found so much love there and I wasn't judged. They prayed for me and cast out demons of depression, suicide, and self-destruction. I went home a changed person. The LORD started to transform my life and the lives of my parents. GOD is faithful and merciful. He forgave my sins and took me in as His child. He took me from a place of death and gave me a new life. Praise the LORD for His transforming power."

Euthanasia is the deliberate ending of a life to relieve pain and suffering. A person who commits suicide, having a clear mind of what they are doing, is committing self-murder. Assisting an individual to commit suicide is also murder. Dr. Jack Kevorkian is well known for his support of euthanasia and has assisted over 100 terminally ill patients to end their lives. Being a health care professional, I have a moral obligation to keep individuals alive, not to end their life. Do not take into your own hands the right that belongs to GOD.

What type of anger do you have?

Have you ever gotten mad at an individual and said terrible things to him/her? Things like "I hate you", "I can't stand you", or "I wish you were dead"? Anger is a very strong emotion that needs to be controlled. The Book of Ephesians warns us of that.

> *"Be angry, and do not sin"; do not let the sun go down on your wrath."*
>
> *- Ephesians 4:26*

There is righteous anger that comes when we witness someone offending GOD or His Word. My husband and I were so upset with Netflix when they promoted a movie featuring JESUS as a homosexual. Our righteous anger moved us to cancel our subscription with them. Righteous anger may also arise when you see people exploited. You can see this in Nehemiah when the nobles and rulers were lending money with an interest and causing their people to go into slavery (Nehemiah 5). GOD's Law prohibited such usury. Deliberate disobedience to the Word of GOD should make you indignant toward the sin, but not the sinner.

Unrighteous anger can bring out the worst of you. Many words are spoken out of anger, words that cannot be taken back. These words have the potential to destroy an individual's self-esteem and confidence. The words you speak can bring blessings to a person's life or they can bring curses (Proverbs 18:21, James 3:8-10). Not only are you cursing another individual, but unrighteous anger also opens a door for a curse to come upon your own life because you have broken the sixth commandment.

> *"You have heard that it was said to those of old, 'You shall not murder, and whoever murders will be in danger of the judgment.' But I say to you that whoever is angry with his brother without a cause shall be in danger of the judgment."*
>
> *- Matthew 5:21-22*

Hatred is another strong emotion whose roots can be very deep. It can drive a person to kill someone. You may not have it in you to kill someone because you know it is wrong, but hatred is also wrong and if you harbor it in your heart, you are violating the sixth commandment. Read about the destructive power words had over the life of Isaac.

"I grew up in an abusive home. My father would tell me that I was the ugliest of my siblings and call me black horse, ugly, and all sorts of names. All these things wounded my heart and I felt very hurt because of the lack of affection. Whenever he mistreated my mother, it would hurt me terribly. One time when he was hitting my mom, I took a broom and split his head, and after that, I promised him that when I got big enough, I would kill him. My heart was full of anger and resentment. From the day I spoke those words, a year had passed, and a terrible thing happened. My father was killed by his best friend. Five hours before my father was killed a prophet of the LORD came to him and warned him that he needed to return to the LORD because his life was in danger and he needed the protection of GOD in his life. My father did not heed the word, and five hours later he was dead.

Even though I hated my father, deep down inside I knew I loved him. I wept so much after his death and swore that I would avenge him. I would fall asleep and awaken contemplating vengeance. I kept hearing a voice telling me I had to pursue the person that killed my father. During this time, my mother had a new boyfriend, and his family was rooted in the faith. They opened their doors to me and adopted me as part of their own family. They took care of me during my adolescence and taught me about JESUS. I went to church the first Sunday staying with this family and the message that the pastor preached on was about forgiveness. That started an internal battle in me. HOLY SPIRIT brought conviction and I knew I needed to forgive. However, the demonic voice that I had been hearing got louder when I would hear the Word of GOD. It would tell me I was a loser and a coward for not avenging my father. It kept telling me that my father was dead and that I would never be able to complete what I had sworn to do. When I would go to church, I would feel so much peace, but I could not forgive. When I left the church, I would hear the voice of the enemy again.

After six months of this turmoil, I cried out to the LORD because I needed to forgive. Immediately I had a personal encounter with Him, and my spirit was broken. I wept bitterly and cried out to the LORD for Him to help me forgive the man that killed my father. At that moment I felt a release, GOD had set me free and I was able to profess that I forgave the man. When I forgave, my entire continence changed, and I felt renewed in my spirit by the LORD.

A month later, I read in the newspaper that the man that killed my father had been killed and cut up into twelve pieces. Rather than rejoicing because justice had been served, I felt such sadness and compassion for him. I knew JESUS had healed me from the hatred I had towards him. I thank the LORD for His mercy on my life and Him setting me free from the anger, resentment, and hatred I harbored in my heart for so long."

The first book of John expresses the Spirit of the Law regarding the sixth commandment. GOD looks at the heart and equates hatred with murder.

> *Whoever hates his brother is a murderer, and you know that no murderer has eternal life abiding in him.*
> *- 1 John 3:15*

By Isaac confessing his sins of hatred and resentment, GOD was able to break the curse off his life and bring the freedom he cried out for.

Are you adding to the wildfire?

Be careful what you say about another individual. It doesn't take much to destroy a person's life. Words can ruin a reputation and if you intend to bring harm to another person's image with no just cause, you are guilty of slander. If you have spoken out of anger, revenge, rebellion, or bitterness, you have disobeyed the sixth commandment.

How do you respond when someone speaks negatively about another individual? Do you participate in the conversation or stay quiet but allow the person to keep talking? By doing so you are participating in gossip. The proper thing to do is to take that person into the Word. The Word of GOD tells us if we have a problem with an individual, we are to go to that person first, and if the individual does not listen, then we are to take witnesses with us the second time (Matthew 18).

> But no man can tame the tongue. It is an unruly evil, full of deadly poison. With it, we bless our God and Father, and with it, we curse men, who have been made in the similitude of God. Out of the same mouth proceed blessing and cursing. My brethren, these things ought not to be so.
>
> - James 3:8-10

It can take years of hard work to build a home, yet one strike of a match can destroy it in minutes. The same is true with one's reputation. A person can take a lifetime building a reputation of honor and integrity, yet a slanderous word can destroy that reputation in a matter of minutes. Once damaged, it is very difficult to repair. Gossip spreads like wildfire. Are you guilty of spreading the wildfire?

How are you treating your temple?

One last area that people overlook when considering murder is their lifestyle choices. As I stated earlier, your body is the temple of HOLY SPIRIT. You have a responsibility before the LORD for taking care of the temple He has blessed you with. How you treat your body today will affect your health and well-being tomorrow. You can add years to your life if you live a healthy lifestyle. However, if you abuse your body with unhealthy eating habits, smoking, consuming alcohol, using illegal drugs, or lack of exercise, you are destroying your body and indirectly killing yourself. Eight of the leading causes of death, both in the United States and worldwide, are caused by poor lifestyle choices and can be preventable.[3] Self-destructive behaviors, if not dealt with, will cause an untimely death. How many people have gone to be with the LORD prematurely?

One of Satan's tactics is to get GOD's people sick, so they are unable to serve. How is your health? Are you eating the right foods? Are you exercising? Are you giving your body the rest it needs? Do all that you can to keep yourself healthy and free from disease. Chapter 11 of Leviticus instructs us on foods permitted and forbidden to eat. If you research these forbidden foods, you will find that they are very unhealthy for you. Use this chapter as a healthy diet guideline so your days can be lengthened.

So many times, we stop the blessing of the LORD. Let your mouth be an avenue of blessings, not curses. Your body is the temple of HOLY SPIRIT, treat it as such. Take care of it and enjoy the blessings of good health as you make wise lifestyle choices.

Questions for Thought
1. What is the difference between killing and murder?
2. What is righteous anger?
3. According to the Word of GOD, when does life begin?
4. How can your tongue cause murder?

Free yourselves of all the subtle tactics the enemy uses to cause you to murder or destroy. Refer to Section 3, Sixth Commandment to continue your process of deliverance.

Chapter 14

ARE YOU KEEPING COVENANT?

Commandment Seven
"You shall not commit adultery."
- Exodus 20:14

The seventh commandment is a commandment that protects covenant. GOD is a God of covenant, you read this throughout the Bible. To reemphasize what we read earlier in this book, a covenant is a formal, solemn, and binding agreement.[1] It is something GOD takes very seriously. GOD established His first covenant with the children of Israel through His covenant with Moses. Under the Mosaic covenant, the Israelites sacrificed animals as sin offerings. However, the shedding of blood through animal sacrifice was insufficient and could not permanently take away sin, nor did it give the people the power to overcome sin. Israel broke their covenant with GOD. But GOD already had a plan to renew His covenant with His people.

> *"Behold, the days are coming, says the LORD, when I will make a new covenant with the house of Israel and with the house of Judah — not according to the covenant that I made with their fathers in the day that I took them by the hand to lead them out of the land of Egypt. My covenant which they broke, though I was a husband to them, says the LORD. But this is the covenant that I will make with the house of Israel after those days, says the LORD: I will put My law in their*

minds, and write it on their hearts; and I will be their God, and they shall be My people."
- Jeremiah 31:31-33

The Hebrew word for new is *chadash* and it means to rebuild, renew repair.[2] It's not that GOD abolished the old covenant, He renewed it and amplified it by replacing the insufficient animal blood sacrifices with the precious blood of His Son. JESUS became the Lamb of GOD who takes away the sins of the world. He paid the ransom price so you can be set free from the slavery of sin.

As JESUS celebrated the Passover meal with His disciples, He took the cup and said, "This is My blood of the new covenant which is shed for many for the remission of sins." The Greek word for new is *kainos* which means to refresh or renew[3]. JESUS didn't abolish the Mosaic Covenant, he intensified it. JESUS's death and resurrection fulfilled the promise of the "new covenant" spoken of by the prophet Jeremiah. Man's relationship with GOD can be reestablished because of GOD's love for us and the giving of His Son as the ultimate sacrifice of all sins.

How do I receive this renewed covenant?

"For this is My blood of the new covenant, which is shed for many for the remission of sins."
- Matthew 26:28

GOD loves you so much that He was willing to allow His Son to die on the cross for the remission of your sins. That was His part of the new covenant. Your part of the new covenant is to accept JESUS as your LORD and Savior. When you accept Him as your LORD and Savior, you enter into a covenant of love with GOD. Your sins are forgiven, and HOLY SPIRIT comes and dwells inside of you. It is HOLY SPIRIT who gives you the power to overcome sin. Your body is now the temple of HOLY SPIRIT and you are part of the bride of Christ. JESUS will one day come back for His bride at His second coming. JESUS fulfilled His part of the covenant. Have you fulfilled yours? Demonstrate your love to Him by engraining GOD's commandments in your mind, writing

146

them on the tablet of your heart, and obeying each one as GOD commands. This is how you demonstrate your love to Him. When you break one of GOD's commandments, you are breaking covenant with Him. Every time Israel sinned and strayed away from GOD, He called them an adulterous nation. When we stray away from the LORD and walk in lawlessness, we are committing spiritual adultery and breaking covenant with Him.

What is GOD's design?

Marriage was ordained by GOD. From the beginning of time, He established marriage according to His plan and design. GOD intended marriage to be a covenant between a man and a woman. This is the only marriage GOD recognizes.

> *Therefore, a man shall leave his father and mother and be joined to his wife, and they shall become one flesh.*
> *- Genesis 2:24*

Becoming one flesh is having a sexual relationship with one another under the covenant of marriage. The seventh commandment is GOD's law to preserve marriage. GOD created His laws to establish His holiness in the marriage and to protect it from harm and destruction. Unfortunately, society has ignored or rejected GOD's laws. Government officials are passing laws contrary to GOD's Word. Many states now recognize same-sex marriage and have laws to protect them. Churches have compromised the Word of GOD and have not only condoned homosexuality but are open to the ordination of people who are gay and lesbian. Contrary to what man may say, marriage is a holy covenant between a man and a woman. Anything contrary to this is sin.

Is there still a death sentence?

GOD intended marriage to be a monogamous and permanent relationship. According to the Old Testament, adultery was punishable with a death sentence.

147

The man who commits adultery with another man's wife, he who commits adultery with his neighbor's wife, the adulterer, and adulteress, shall surely be put to death.
- Leviticus 20:10

The punishment for breaking this law was death by stoning. The death sentence is still present today but manifesting in different ways. Adultery destroys marriages and relationships. Homicides are on the rise because of jealousy and rage. Abortions are by the thousands because of unwanted babies conceived through sexual promiscuity. Pedophile victims end up being killed and dumped as trash. Sexually transmitted diseases (STDs) are at an all high. An estimated 770,000 people died from AIDS-related illnesses in 2018[4].

Do you not know that the unrighteous will not inherit the kingdom of God? Do not be deceived. Neither fornicators, nor idolaters, no adulterers, nor homosexuals, nor sodomites, nor thieves, nor covetous, nor drunkards, nor revilers, nor extortioners will inherit the kingdom of God.
- 1 Corinthians 6:9-10

GOD's Word warns us not to be deceived. Tragically, Christians deceive themselves into thinking that GOD does not require them to live in holiness. This is far from the truth and if there is no repentance, you will lose your eternal inheritance and face eternal judgment in hell. What a death sentence that would be. If you are struggling with sexual immorality, the LORD can set you free. Rebecca was a victim of incest. The following is her testimony of how GOD brought healing and deliverance to her life.

"I was molested as a child by my grandfather. This incestuous relationship continued from the time I was eight years old until my early 20's. My grandfather gave me an STD called genital herpes at the age of 19. I started getting ulcers in my genital area and went to a clinic and that's when I was told of my diagnosis. They did a culture and sent it to the agency that handles STD's in Puerto Rico and I became another statistic. The clinic asked about my sexual relationships to determine who infected me and if I passed it on to anyone else. I lied because I didn't want anyone to know about my grandfather, nor did I want to get him in trouble. I was told this virus was incurable and that I would continue having episodes of herpes outbreaks for the rest of my life.

I was in my 30's when I gave my life to JESUS. I struggled with guilt and shame for years, even as a believer, and kept falling into fornication. As time passed, I started attending an apostolic church that introduced me to the ministry of deliverance. I was ministered to in the area of sexual impurity due to the incest in my life. I was able to forgive my grandfather and myself. I was free from the guilt and shame that had been there for most of my life. GOD not only delivered me from demons of sexual impurity, but He also healed me of genital herpes as well. Since my deliverance, which is over twenty years ago, there has not been an outbreak of herpes. I am not tempted with sexual impurity any longer and have kept myself pure. My relationship with the LORD continues to grow. Because of my obedience and keeping my focus on Him, the LORD has brought a wonderful Christian man into my life. We are making plans for our wedding day. Until then, we are keeping ourselves pure so we can enjoy the blessings of entering a covenant with holiness. I thank the LORD for restoring my life."

GOD moved powerfully in the life of Rebecca. She found the strength to forgive her grandfather, she was delivered from a spirit of sexual impurity, and she was miraculously healed. After her deliverance and healing, she kept her eyes focused on JESUS. Because of her obedience, the LORD has brought a godly man into her life. What a beautiful testimony.

Genetics or Spiritual?

Science would have you believe that genetics is a determinant of homosexual and lesbian behavior. However, there have been many individuals bound in this type of lifestyle who have been delivered from their bondage and living a healthy heterosexual lifestyle. The root of homosexuality and lesbianism is spiritual bondage. The following testimony supports this belief.

"Maria is an identical twin who came for deliverance. She and her identical twin sister were victims of incest. As Maria grew older, she fell into lesbianism. Her identical twin, however, did not. Rather, she succumbed to the sin of fornication. Identical twins have the same genetic make-up. If lesbianism and homosexuality were caused by a genetic defect, both twins should have fallen into lesbianism. The iniquity of sexual immorality stemming from her generational line is what caused the lesbianism in Maria. Iniquity is the deep root of sin and if it is not uprooted, it will continue to grow throughout your generations to come. Maria became a Christian and sought deliverance. She was prayed for and demons were rebuked from her. The iniquity of sexual immorality was broken. To this day she is free and happily married to her husband."

Even though society accepts homosexuality and lesbianism, this acceptance is contrary to the Word of GOD.

For this reason, God gave them up to vile passions. For even their women exchanged the natural use for what is against nature. Likewise, also the men, leaving the natural use of the woman, burned in their lust for one another, men with men committing what is shameful, and receiving in themselves the penalty of their error which was due.

- Romans 1:26-27

You shall not lie with a male as with a woman. It is an abomination.

- Leviticus 18:22

An abomination is the Bible's strongest expression of hatred for wickedness. The scripture is very clear. GOD detests the sin of homosexuality and lesbianism. If you are bound by this demonic behavior, know that GOD loves you, and wants to see you set free. It is very difficult to overcome this on your own. Seek help and obtain your freedom today.

Are you defiling GOD's temple?

The letter of the Law of this commandment states "You shall not commit adultery". Adultery is committed when a married individual has a sexual encounter with someone other than their spouse. However, the Spirit of the Law of this commandment entails much more than just adultery.

"You have heard that it was said to those of old, 'You shall not commit adultery.' But I say to you that whoever looks at a woman to lust for her has already committed adultery with her in his heart."

- Matthew 5:27-28

Even if you have not had a sexual relationship with another, you can still be guilty of adultery. The sin begins in your heart. You can commit adultery through your emotions. If you are looking or thinking of an individual other than your spouse, and it causes you to have a strong sexual desire, you are guilty.

This commandment does not just address the breaking of a marriage covenant. It encompasses all areas of sexual immorality. Sexual activity outside of the covenant of marriage is a sin. Many will say that this is old fashion, get with the times.

Just because living together outside of marriage is the norm, doesn't make it right. I was once told that I was judging when I told an individual that she was in sin. I'm not judging, the Word of GOD is judging the behavior. The temptation to engage in sexual immorality can easily overpower your self-control. That is why the Word of GOD tells us to escape from it.

> *Flee sexual immorality. Every sin that a man does is outside the body, but he who commits sexual immorality sins against his own body. Or do you not know that your body is the temple of the Holy Spirit who is in you, whom you have from God, and you are not your own?*
>
> *- 1 Corinthians 6:18-19*

You are the temple of HOLY SPIRIT, keep yourself pure and holy so the LORD will continue to fill you with more of His presence and anointing. When you commit sexual immorality, you are defiling GOD's temple and insulting HOLY SPIRIT. Sin separates you from GOD so when you fall into sexual immorality, it hinders your relationship with Him and destroys your spiritual life. According to the National Institute of Health, microscopic tears occur during sexual intercourse[5]. The friction that occurs during intercourse will cause microscopic tearing in the vagina and the tip of the penis. In the spiritual realm, you are establishing a blood covenant with your partner. Not only that, any demons that are plaguing your sexual partner will also be transmitted to you as you engage in sexual immorality (1 Corinthians 6:16). When going through a process of deliverance renounce any blood covenant you established through sexual contact.

What's the harm?

A new national survey of Christian men reveals shocking statistics about high rates of pornography use and addiction, plus rampant sexual infidelity among married Christian men. Ninety-five percent admit that they have viewed pornography and fifty-four percent look at porn at least once a month.[6] With the availability of pornography on the Internet, is it any wonder individuals have difficulty overcoming the temptation. With the shocking statistics of Christian men addicted, why is this sin rarely addressed at the pulpit? Sexual relations under the covenant of marriage is a gift from GOD, but Satan has twisted it, replacing it with lust, fornication, adultery, incest, pornography, rape, and all forms of perversion.

Pornography may seem harmless, but it is not. Pornography is nothing but exploitation. Individuals are used as sex objects to satisfy the lust of people they don't even know. It is very addictive, hard to break, and damages the mind and soul. When exposed, pornography brings emotional and psychological damage to the spouse and children of the offender. The spouse feels betrayed and loses trust in the offender. Here is a testimony of Thomas. He speaks on his addiction to pornography and the spiral downfall it took him.

"For the past ten years of my life, I have been addicted to pornography. The pornography began with heterosexual couples but later turned to homosexual pornography. I never saw myself as handsome, successful, falling in love, or getting married, and having a family. I had very low self-esteem and hated myself. I was suicidal from the ages of 11 – 17 and many times attempted to take my life through shooting myself, overdosing on alcohol and pills, and cutting myself, but was unsuccessful. I was never really attracted to women or even confident enough to approach them. I found that very passive gay men were more accepting of me and found I could be a man through their passiveness. By the age of 24, I slept with over 40 men and had many scares of HIV/AIDS. I lived in homeless shelters, in my car, and even on the streets. I did anything to survive. I became numb to who I was through drugs, witchcraft, and alcohol. The devil had convinced me that this was my punishment for all that I had done to my family and friends over the years.

I felt myself slipping down a dark hole, with nothing to grab onto. The sad part was that I was going to church, calling people hypocrites and liars, while the night before I was with someone I had just met at a club or online. I stole money, clothes, jewelry, and even credit cards. I used sex for money, drugs, and favors to get ahead in life.

All that changed when I accepted an invitation from a long-time teen friend to go to a church service. I brought with me, my male companion. As I listened to the preaching, the only word I heard was "Enough." I knew GOD was speaking to me. The words kept ringing through my mind and heart. I knew it was a day of decision to turn my life around. I went to the altar and reconciled myself with the LORD. I was broken before Him and willing to do whatever I needed to find my freedom. I told my male companion we could no longer be together.

The following night my long-time friend took me to her church. The pastor of that church was a famous musician in the '70s and most of the members of the worship team had experienced some type of abuse. They welcomed me with open arms. Through prayer, fasting, deliverance, and much meditating on GOD's Word, I began to allow GOD to be the LORD of my life. It was in this same church that I was able to approach a woman for the first time. She was a beautiful lady inside and out. She knew about my past and was able to overlook it because of the transformation she had seen in my life."

What a powerful testimony of the redeeming power of JESUS. Thomas's relationship with Liza grew and they were planning to get married. However, something traumatic happened. One Sunday Thomas led all three worship services. That evening the worship team went out for a bite to eat. Thomas came home late and went to bed. The next day his parents found him lying lifeless in his bed. The medical examiner could not determine the cause of death. The cause of death on his death certificate read "undetermined". Had Thomas not repented of his homosexual lifestyle and allowed GOD to be LORD of his life again, he would have spent eternity in hell. Praise GOD he repented before it was too late.

Why is masturbation wrong?

Some Christians believe that because masturbation doesn't harm anyone, it is not a sin. Although there is no specific scripture that mentions masturbation, there are scriptures that indicate it is sin. Transsexualism and pornography are not mentioned in the Bible, yet you know how demonic they are. Look at the spirits behind the behaviors, ask HOLY SPIRIT to show you what the spirit of this law includes.

> *Therefore, a man shall leave his father and mother and be joined to his wife, and they shall become one flesh.*
> *- Genesis 2:24*

A husband and wife are to become one flesh. That was the original design of a sexual relationship. It is a beautiful expression of love from GOD for those under the covenant of marriage. Anything differing from this is sin. Masturbation is self-centered and self-gratifying. As one is masturbating, the individual has sexual fantasies. Many times, it becomes a compulsive behavior. Lustful desires are the root of this gratifying behavior. Any behavior that satisfies your lust is a sin.

> *For all that is in the world — the lust of the flesh, the lust of the eyes, and the pride of life — is not of the Father but is of the world. And the world is passing away, and the lust of it; but he who does the will of God abides forever.*
> *- 1 John 2:16-17*

Masturbation is Satan's way of distorting a sexual pleasure intended to be enjoyed under covenant with your spouse. Some will argue that masturbation is better than fornicating or adultery. Masturbation will not fulfill your sexual pleasures, consequently, it will prompt you to masturbate even more. Many individuals will masturbate while looking at pornography. These two behaviors have a strong bond with each other. Both are very addictive and difficult to break, especially with the powerful hormonal and psychological elements of masturbation.[7] The only way to overcome this compulsiveness is to confess your sin, seek deliverance, and ask HOLY SPIRIT to take control of your life. It is only through the power of HOLY SPIRIT that you can break the power of the flesh and overcome this sin.

> I say then: Walk in the Spirit, and you shall not fulfill the lust of the flesh.
>
> - Galatians 5:16

What else is an open door?

The lifestyle portrayed by soap operas has no value to the spirit-filled Christian. Each episode is filled with adultery, fornication, hatred, and deception. Watching these types of shows often leads one to have sexual fantasies and it opens the door to sensuality. Be careful of what you watch, the jokes you tell, and the words you speak and listen to. If any of these have sexual implications attached to them, avoid them. If you engage in flirting, stop. These are all ways the enemy disguises sin.

Be careful about how you dress. Dressing in a sensuous way draws attention to one's body. The spirit of Jezebel is a controlling spirit working through the lust of the flesh and sensuality. If you struggle with sensuality, consider the possibility that Jezebel is at work in your life. Women need to be careful wearing garments that show cleavage. Although this is not dressing in a sensuous way, it may be a stumbling block for those who struggle with sexual thoughts and fantasies. You cannot allow yourself to be a stumbling block to those who are weak.

Your covenant with GOD is vital. Blessings of protection and provision will follow those who establish and maintain a covenant relationship with the LORD. Don't lose out on the blessings GOD has for your life when you walk in obedience.

Questions for Thought
1. How did the Israelites break their covenant with GOD in the Old Testament?
2. How were sins taken away in the Old Testament?
3. What did JESUS mean when He spoke, "This is My blood of the new covenant"?
4. What is spiritual adultery?
5. What is GOD's original design for marriage?

Free yourself of all the twisted tactics the enemy uses to cause you to break covenant with GOD and/or covenant with your spouse. Refer to Section 3, Seventh Commandment to continue your process of deliverance.

Chapter 15
ARE YOU SURE IT'S YOURS?

Commandment Eight
"You shall not steal."
- Exodus 20:15

Most people work hard for what they have. Unfortunately, some people take what doesn't belong to them and have no remorse for it. The eighth commandment was established to protect private property. No one has the right to take your property unlawfully. From the beginning of mankind, stealing has been one of man's downfalls. The very first sin ever committed was stealing. GOD told Adam and Eve they could eat of every tree of the garden except for the tree of the knowledge of good and evil. In disobedience, they took that which did not belong to them and ate of the fruit. Because of their sin, they were kicked out of the Garden of Eden and required to work for their food. The sinful nature of Adam and Eve has been passed on from generation to generation.

After Joshua led the Israelites into the promised land, the first sin committed was stealing. Achan committed a trespass regarding the accursed things. They were things that GOD commanded to be destroyed, but Achan coveted those items and stole them. The seventh chapter of Joshua explains how Joshua and his army were defeated in the Battle of Ai. This was a battle that should have easily been won. Their defeat was a result of one man's sin. Achan's actions did not just affect himself, they affected an entire army. The defeat at Ai was a strong statement,

GOD does not tolerate sin and would no longer be with Israel until the sin in the camp was removed. That is why they were defeated.

So, the LORD said to Joshua: "Get up! Why do you lie thus on your face? Israel has sinned, and they have also transgressed My covenant which I commanded them. For they have even taken some of the accursed things and have both stolen and deceived; and they have also put it among their own stuff."
- Joshua 7:10-11

GOD's anger arose because Israel failed to keep their covenant with Him. He takes very seriously His covenant. When you disobey GOD, expect consequences. Not only was Achan punished for his sin, but his entire family was also stoned to death. Nations are under a curse because of the iniquity of exploitation and corruption that infiltrates their land.

At what cost?

Today we live in a society with the mentality of getting rich quickly at all costs, even if it means obtaining it dishonestly. Stealing has become an epidemic and a way of life in America. People take belongings of others with no regard for the rights and feelings of those they victimize. You hear time and time again of individuals who have been fooled by get-rich-quick schemes, the elderly who have been taken unfair advantage of, con-artists preying on the naïve, and manufacturers who misleadingly advertise their products. Identity theft is on the rise, especially in credit card theft. An individual can spend many years building their credit and reputation, only to have it ruined because someone has stolen their identity. Each of these tactics is preying on the innocent and a form of stealing. If you have obtained money or material possessions through deception or unlawful gain, you have sinned against GOD and broken His commandment. There are two rightful ways of obtaining possessions: by honest work and as a gift from GOD through another individual. Gaining possessions through any other means is sin and the root of that sin is selfishness and greed fed by the spirit of mammon.

Stealing opens the door for the enemy to accuse you. It also opens the door for curses to come upon your life, especially in your finances. When you steal, the judgment of GOD will come upon you sooner or later because you have placed a curse upon yourself.

> Then he said to me, "This is the curse that goes out over the face of the whole earth: 'Every thief shall be expelled,' according to this side of the scroll; and, 'every perjurer shall be expelled,' according to that side of it. I will send out the curse," says the LORD of hosts; "It shall enter the house of the thief and the house of the one who swears falsely by My name. It shall remain in the midst of his house and consume it, with its timber and stone."
>
> - Zechariah 5:3-4

Our government categorizes theft as a felony or a misdemeanor, depending on the value stolen. Individuals who take something of little value will say, "It's no big deal, it wasn't worth much", and take lightly their actions. Some don't even consider it stealing. There is no such thing as petty theft. In GOD's eyes stealing is stealing no matter how big or small. Adam and Eve took a piece of fruit and they paid a huge price for the consequences of their sin. They were kicked out of the Garden of Eden. Call it as it is! Stealing is sin, no matter what the size.

As a Christian, you may be self-conscious that stealing is wrong. However, there may be some actions you don't consider as being wrong, yet the Word of GOD would differ. These subtle behaviors could be stopping the financial blessings GOD has for your life. Let's uncover the less obvious forms of stealing.

Are you giving what belongs to GOD?

The first area to address is stealing from GOD, whether out of ignorance or out of rebellion and disobedience. Many believe tithing is an option. This is not what the Word of GOD says.

'And all the tithe of the land, whether of the seed of the land or of the fruit of the tree, is the LORD's. It is holy to the LORD.'

- Leviticus 27:30

You are commanded to give ten percent of your earnings to the LORD. That is what a tithe is, yet many do not feel obligated to do so. Some say they can't afford that. You can't afford not to! Individuals will share with me that they just can't seem to get ahead, every time they turn around something is happening to drain their finances. Does this sound like you? The first question I ask them is, "Are you tithing?" When you don't tithe, it opens the door for the adversary to bring an accusation against you and curses to come upon your finances.

"Will a man rob God? Yet you have robbed Me! But you say, 'In what way have we robbed You?' In tithes and offerings. You are cursed with a curse, for you have robbed Me, even this whole nation. Bring all the tithes into the storehouse, that there may be food in My house, and try Me now in this," says the LORD of hosts, "If I will not open for you the windows of heaven and pour out for you such blessing that there will not be room enough to receive it."

- Malachi 3:8-10

This is one commandment the LORD tells you to try Him. GOD is testing your faith. I have seen in my own life the faithfulness of GOD when I put Him first and trust Him as my Provider. Giving to the LORD is a form of worship and it demonstrates your faithfulness and trust in Him. Giving to the LORD demonstrates your gratitude for what He has done in your life. It is an attitude of the heart. Do you give reluctantly or solely give to get something in return? If so, this wrongful attitude of tithing is not pleasing to GOD. Giving to Him needs to come from a pure heart of worship, expecting nothing in return.

Honor the Lord *with your possessions, and with the firstfruits of all your increase; so, your barns will be filled with plenty, and your vats will overflow with new wine.*
- Proverbs 3:9-10

The first portion that comes out of your paycheck should be the Lord's tithe. Some will pay their bills and if there is anything left over, give to the Lord. He does not want your leftovers. He wants the first fruit of your paycheck. It is easy to tithe when you are in abundance, but are you able to tithe when the budget is tight? Here is Molly's testimony.

"For many years I had been faithful in giving of my tithes and offerings. I was gainfully employed and was financially in a position where I could give liberally, but then an unexpected shift came. I lost my job and for the first time in many years, I found myself trying to figure out how I was going to pay my bills and feed my family. Deep down I knew God would take care of me, and he would provide, but I lost sight of my responsibility to the covenant I had with God with my finances. Whether I had or didn't have, I was not to rob God. My immediate need blinded me of the requirement of honoring God in my lack as much as I had honored him through times of abundance. In my desperation, I stopped tithing.

Initially, I skated along in the mercy of the Lord, and I told myself and God that when I started working again, I would pay back what I owed in tithes. God was faithful in providing the job, but I was not faithful in paying my debt to the Lord. Once I started working again, I began to tell myself that I needed to catch up on all my bills first, and then I would square up with the Lord. This opened a huge door for the enemy in my life, and it moved me from being under the protection and blessing of God to be under the curse of God. This open door led to a spirit of confusion and craziness to come over my life, and the heavy hand of God's judgment was upon me because of it. The Lord allowed a spirit of craziness to visit me and torment me. There were a couple of months that I wasn't even in my right mind. I began to have suicidal thoughts, and evil thoughts would visit me throughout the day and night. I had no peace during this time. It wasn't until I fell on my face before GOD and repented, that His hand of judgment relented. I felt led by HOLY SPIRIT to present a "peace offering" to the LORD to restore the heart of GOD, and I have been faithfully tithing and presenting offerings ever since. I thank the LORD that His mercy triumphed over His judgment in my life, and I'm thankful to be under His blessing and not under His curse."

When you fail to tithe, you are demonstrating a lack of faith and trust in GOD. If you want to be in a position where GOD can fully bless you, understand the value of tithing. Tithing is your investment in heaven, and no one can steal that investment from you. If you are faithful with your tithes and offerings, GOD will continue to bless you. You can never out-give the LORD. I know of an individual who tithed what she received from her food stamps. She would give a portion of the food to a homeless person or someone in dire need every month while she received food stamp assistance. To this day she has never lacked.

Many see prosperity as being able to buy whatever they want or having a huge bank account. This is the opposite of Kingdom prosperity. The LORD wants to prosper you so you can be a blessing to others and help those in need. It is good to save for the future, but if that is your primary focus, you are missing a godly principle that can richly bless your life.

Have you cheated on the government?

Just as you are to tithe, you are also expected to pay your taxes, even if you don't like it. The Word of GOD does not say to pay taxes only if they are fair or if the taxes are used appropriately. You are not responsible for what others do, but you are responsible for obeying the law and obeying GOD's Word.

> *"Tell us, therefore, what do You think? Is it lawful to pay taxes to Caesar, or not?" But Jesus perceived their wickedness, and said, "Why do you test Me, you hypocrites? Show Me the tax money." So, they brought Him a denarius. And He said to them, "Whose image and inscription is this?" They said to Him, "Caesar's." And He said to them, "Render therefore to Caesar the things that are Caesar's and to God the things that are God's."*
>
> *- Matthew 22:17-21*

> *Therefore, you must be subject, not only because of wrath but also for conscience' sake. For because of this you also pay taxes, for they are God's ministers attending continually to this very thing. Render therefore to all their due: taxes to whom taxes are due, customs to whom customs, fear to whom fear, honor to whom honor.*
>
> *- Romans 13:5-7*

Unless it contradicts GOD's Word, you are to submit to your governmental authorities. When you submit to those GOD has placed in authority over you, you are honoring GOD. The Bible is very specific. As Christians you have a moral and civil obligation to pay taxes, you also have a Biblical responsibility. When you do not claim all your earnings or stretch the truth when filing your income taxes, you are stealing from the government.

"Ruby called me asking for advice. She stated her finances were a mess and have been for some time. She has worked hard for the past six months and has nothing to show for it. She then shared the open door to the curses on her finances. She has a condominium that she has rented for the past six years but has never claimed that as income on her tax returns. Her financial adviser has told her she needs to fix this because if the Internal Revenue Service (IRS) discovers this, she could end up paying a huge penalty and more than likely charge her interest for the past six years for any increase in her adjusted income. This has brought a lot of concern and fear in her life. Some nights she will have horrible dreams, other nights she is unable to sleep."

Ruby didn't need my advice. She knew in her heart what she needed to do. The truth is the only thing that will set her free from the fear, guilt, and accusations the enemy has over her. Doing what is right will cancel the curse she is experiencing with her finances. She ended the conversation by saying she was going to make an appointment with her financial adviser so he can guide her in taking the necessary steps needed to correct her taxes. Hopefully, she follows through and does what is right before the LORD.

Another way of stealing from the government are through disability fraud. Exaggerating a medical problem that could potentially be disabling is a fraud. Individuals who legitimately receive government disability for a medical condition must report any medical improvement to the government. If they do not report the improvement and continue to receive disability payments, they are stealing from the government.

The welfare system has become a two-edged sword. It is a government program that assists individuals and families in need. This is where the welfare system has become a blessing. Capable individuals are expected to receive training or take the needed steps towards financial independence. Unfortunately, it has become a way of life for many. Some choose not to work because they have become comfortable with their freestyle way of living and are too lazy to find a job and make an honest day's wages.

If you work or earn any wages while receiving unemployment insurance benefits, you must report these wages. If you do not, it is a criminal offense. You are stealing from the government. Those who receive unemployment usually receive food stamps as well. You can also commit food stamp fraud by intentionally withholding information on an application so that you receive additional public assistance or food stamp benefits. If your family income increases while receiving food stamp benefits, you should report the increase to the welfare agency. If you do not report the change, you could be stealing if your increased income disqualifies you from getting food stamps or decreases the amount of assistance you are entitled to.

It's all in a day's work, or is it?

The workplace is another area where honesty and justice are tested. Labor trafficking and exploitation happen every day. If you have ever hired someone to do work for you, whether for a business or a personal need, and you did not pay them a fair hourly rate, you have taken advantage of and exploited them and that is contrary to the Word of God.

> *"You shall not oppress a hired servant who is poor and needy, whether one of your brethren or one of the aliens who is in your land within your gates. Each day you shall give him his wages, and not let the sun go down on it, for he is poor and has set his heart on it; lest he cry out against you to the LORD, and it be sin to you."*
> *- Deuteronomy 24:14-15*

> *Indeed, the wages of the laborer who mowed your fields, which you kept back by fraud, cry out; and the cries of the reapers have reached the ears of the LORD of Sabbath.*
> *- James 5:4*

The cries of injustice do not go unheard. God hears the cries of those being exploited and those participating in exploitation will be judged.

Some will fake an injury just so they can claim worker's compensation, yet they can do all kinds of work around the house. This is fraud and you are stealing when you make false claims. The Chamber of Commerce estimates 75% of employees steal from the workplace. An estimated $50 billion is stolen annually from US businesses by employees.[1] Personnel are prosecuted for taking items without paying for them or pocketing money from the cash register. You may think that you have never stolen from your employer because you have never participated in these actions, but you may be fooling yourself.

One of the most common types of employee theft is stealing time from your employer. Have you come to work late or left work early? Many individuals will have coworkers punch them in or out when they are not at work. Do you eat your lunch at your desk and then turn around and take a lunch hour? Do you take frequent coffee breaks or excessive break times? Do you use company time to take care of personal business? How much time do you spend socializing with coworkers? These examples may seem insignificant to you, but the time adds up. If you spend ten minutes checking your e-mail or Facebook page every couple of hours, you are stealing hours of paid time from your employer. Some individuals go as far as to thoughtlessly operate their business during working hours. Your employer trusts you to do a day's work. Falling short of this is stealing the trust of your employer and robbing him/her of wages that you did not earn.

And whatever you do in word or deed, do all in the name of the Lord Jesus, giving thanks to God the Father through Him.

- Colossians 3:17

As Christians, your character should reflect good working ethics. Others should see you as hardworking, dependable, and honest. Your actions should reflect the characteristics of JESUS. Does your work ethics bring glory to Him? Taking company pens, using company paper for personal use, printing, or using the copying machine for personal use without asking are all examples of other ways employees steal from their employers. These examples may seem petty and you may be saying to yourself, "The company can afford it." These petty items add up and if one could calculate the total cost of petty theft from each employee per month, you would be surprised at the amount.

What right do you have?

There is much confusion and misunderstanding when it comes to digital music and CD/DVD copying. Singers and composers put much time and effort to produce a CD or DVD. The U.S. Copyright Act of 1976 was established to protect authors, musicians, artists, etc. of their creative work. Webster's Dictionary defines copyright as the exclusive legal right to reproduce, publish, sell, or distribute the matter and form of something.[2] Making copies and distributing them freely is depriving the artists of their rightful earnings. Receiving a copy of a CD/DVD from someone else makes you just as guilty as the one who made the copy.

The Bible clearly states that the laborer is worthy of his wages (Luke 10:7). Downloading videos containing copyrighted songs from YouTube and storing them on your computer is another copyright invasion. Unless you see a "free download" link displayed with a song, it is illegal to download. Don't stop at just CDs. Unauthorized copying of pictures, images, software, or written materials constitutes copyright theft. Software piracy is very common in many countries. This has opened the door to bring a curse of poverty upon the land. If you have obtained any type of software illegally, remove it from your computer. Destroy any copies of CD's or DVD's you do not have legal rights to.

Whose work is it?

Have you ever gotten credit for something that someone else did? How did you respond? If you don't correct the situation, you are stealing credit from another individual. As a former teacher, I would constantly catch students trying to cheat on an exam. Individuals who cheat are stealing knowledge from another individual and pretending it is theirs. I also encountered students plagiarizing their essays. They would turn in the work, pretending it was their writing. Any time you use another source and do not give the individual credit, you are stealing the credit of that individual. I know of a teacher who received praise from

168

their principal for a teaching strategy that another teacher had given her. She received the praise, acting as if it were her original idea. When her coworker found out, she was upset that she didn't tell the principal where she got the idea and their relationship was never the same.

When is borrowing wrong?

I'm sure all of us can say we have borrowed money or an item from time to time. That's what family and friends are for, to help when in a bind. If you borrow with the pretense of paying it back, you should return what was borrowed as quickly as possible. If borrowing is the norm, you are living above your income and that is wrong. The use of credit cards brings instant gratification, impulsive buying, and spending more than you can afford. Many get so far in debt and they are not able to climb their way out of it. The Bible warns against such borrowing.

> *The rich rules over the poor and the borrower is servant to the lender.*
>
> *- Proverbs 22:7*

> *The wicked borrows and does not repay, but the righteous shows mercy and gives.*
>
> *- Psalms 37:21*

I know of an individual who charged her credit card to the max with no intention of paying anything back. Creditors were calling her constantly and she never answered the phone. I asked her if she was concerned and she stated "No, it will be on my credit record for seven years, after that it will go away". This is wrong and deceiving. When you buy on credit, you are promising to pay back what you have borrowed. Anything short of that is stealing. If you borrow, it is under the pretense of returning what was lent to you. If you borrow and do not return, you are stealing. You have indirectly taken something that does not belong to you.

Have you replaced what you damaged?

When you accidentally break or damage something that does not belong to you, you should replace the damaged item. If not, you have stolen because the owner no longer has the item in their possession. The individual may tell you there's no need to replace it. However, you should pray about it and let your heart be your guide. Maliciously damaging another person's belongings is vandalism and a crime. Innocent people work hard for what they have, only to have it intentionally damage by spiteful people. This is wrong and restitution needs to be made. If you have done this in the past, you need to ask the LORD how to restore the individual you victimized.

Are you a thief in disguise?

Retailers are not the only victim when shoplifting occurs. We become victims because it drives the retail prices higher and we the consumers are paying for it. Retail theft has many disguises: changing price tags on items, returning clothing after it has been worn and refund fraud are just a few. I have heard of ladies buying a dress for a wedding or prom, only to return it after wearing it for the event. Some have the nerve to shoplift items from a store and return them the next day, stating they lost the sales slip. Have you ever found an empty candy wrapper left on one of the store shelves, knowing that the individual who ate it more than likely did not pay for it? Have you ever gone to a fast-food store to buy a drink from the fountain, fill it, take a few swallows out of the cup, and then refill it with more drink before paying for it? If there are no free refills, you have just stolen from the retailer. While on vacation have you ever taken a towel home as a souvenir?

A friend told me she was ministering one day to a new believer. They met at a local restaurant to have a Bible study over lunch. This individual grabbed a handful of sugar packets to place them in her purse as they were getting up to leave. My friend used this as an opportunity to teach her that what she was doing was wrong. Taking condiments from a restaurant may seem trivial, but it is breaking the eighth commandment. So is using a Satellite dish to steal electronic signals or using a cable connection to your house which you have not paid for. All these examples are ways the enemy will disguise stealing. They may seem petty, but in GOD's eyes, they are dishonest. Don't fall into the snares of the adversary.

How honest are you?

Have you ever come out of a store, checked your receipt, and found a mistake to your benefit? What do you do? Once I was shopping at Jo-Ann Fabrics. I was buying numerous items, including thirty-three packets of elastic for a special project. When I got to my car and was looking through the receipt, I noticed I was only charged for three packets of elastic. I went back into the store and informed them of their mistake. They thanked me for my honesty and said most people would not have done that. On another occasion, I was buying a sweater and scarf at Kohls. I had placed the scarf around the hanger of the sweater. When the gentleman at the register rang me up, he only charged me for the sweater. I told him he forgot to charge me for the scarf. He was thinking the two were a set. Because of my honesty, he gave me a 20% discount. Had I not said anything in each of these situations, I would have been stealing. Some may think, "Oh, well it was their mistake." Yes, it was their mistake, but you don't correct a wrong with another wrong. In GOD's eyes, you are stealing. I don't want any open doors where the enemy, Satan can bring accusations to stop the blessings GOD has for my finances.

Where is your trust?

GOD is the one who provided you with a job. When you take His provision and gamble it away, you are being poor stewards of His money. Many Christians see gambling as harmless, especially when they are only spending a dollar here or there for a lottery ticket or buying a raffle ticket for a needy cause. People will justify their need to play the lottery by saying the money goes towards education or another good cause. Even though you use these excuses, the underlying reason for gambling is the hopes of getting something in return. Many see it as a get rich quick opportunity. Those that win, covet to win more. Those that lose play in hopes to win back what they lost. What a vicious cycle! What seemed like a harmless $10 lottery ticket has now turned into compulsive gambling and addiction that can be difficult to break unless the LORD intervenes.

> *Trust in the LORD with all your heart and lean not on your own understanding.*
> *- Proverbs 3:5*

Gambling is stealing because it is taking money from a household that should be used to meet the needs of the family. Children lack clothing and food because of parents spending their earnings carelessly or compulsively on gambling. People who gamble put their trust in luck rather than putting their trust in GOD. Put your trust in the LORD and see the ways He will bless your life.

If something is stopping the blessing over your finances, hopefully, this chapter has revealed the root. If it hasn't, ask GOD to show you any open doors that have brought curses to your finances. GOD desires to see His people blessed and prosperous.

Questions for Thought
1. How does GOD see tithing?
2. What does "Render therefore to Caesar the things that are Caesar's, and to GOD the things that are GOD's" mean?
3. Why is playing the lottery wrong?
4. How can you oppress a hired servant?
5. What are subtle ways of stealing from your employer?

Free yourself of every subtle way the enemy uses to cause you to take what doesn't belong to you. Refer to Section 3, Eighth Commandment to continue your process of deliverance.

Chapter 16
WHAT WEB ARE YOU MAKING?

Commandment Nine
"You shall not bear false witness against your neighbor."
- Exodus 20:16

The ninth commandment speaks of truth and is one of the most often broken of the commandments. Wouldn't it be wonderful if you could take people at their word and believe everything they say? Think of how different this world would be if people would do what they say and keep their promises. Lying has become a way of life and unfortunately, Christians are not immune to it and have been sucked into this whirlwind of deception. Don't be deceived, Satan is the father of lies and you should not accept lying as normal. This is far from the truth and breaking this commandment is going totally against the characteristic of who GOD is.

> *"God is not a man, that He should lie, nor a son of man, that He should repent."*
>
> *- Numbers 23:19*

JESUS described himself as the Way, the Truth, and the Life (John 14:6). JESUS's reputation was such that people knew He was a man of His word. If you are an imitator of JESUS, speak the truth. When you come to salvation, you are to put off the deeds of the flesh and walk according to the Spirit. You may believe that little white lies are harmless and perfectly acceptable. However, GOD's Word tells us differently.

> *Lying lips are an abomination to the LORD, but those who deal truthfully are His delight.*
>
> *- Proverbs 12:22*

How is your reputation? Do people believe the words you speak? Can you be described as an individual with integrity? I would hope so. Mark Twain once said, "If you tell the truth, you don't have to remember anything." Most people who lie unknowing set up a trap for themselves. They build a lie upon another lie and eventually get caught in their web of lies, not remembering what was spoken in the first place.

What is the root?

If you know that lying is sinning against GOD, why do you so easily fall prey to it? Why has lying become so natural that you don't even think twice about doing it? Fear drives people to fabricate lies. When you have done something wrong, you fear the consequences if the truth is exposed. You cover up your mistakes with a blanket of lies. You fear what others may think if the truth is uncovered. You stretch the truth or tell lies to protect your self-image. You don't tell the truth because of your fears of inadequacy or insecurity.

> *The fear of man lays a snare, but whoever trusts in the LORD is safe.*
>
> *- Proverbs 29:25*

Yielding to fear shows your lack of trust in GOD. If you put your trust in GOD and approach Him with a repentant heart, He will see you through even when you have done something wrong. Telling the truth in difficult situations takes courage, self-discipline, and faith. If you persevere in telling the truth you will build character and become a stronger individual.

Pride is another root cause of lying. You want to look good in the eyes of others, so you puff yourself up with flattering words. You are so prideful and concerned about what people will think that you are willing to lie to make yourself appear better than who you are. Here is a testimony of Anthony who had a deep root of lying and pride.

"I remember when I was about six years old, having a conversation with a cousin and one of my aunts. We were talking about poor children who live on the streets. My aunt was trying to show my cousin and me the importance of showing compassion for those children. I proceeded to tell my aunt that my father bought a lot of food and gave it to the poor on numerous occasions. It was a big lie and I would make up stories all the time, just to make myself look good.

As a teenager, I started serving the LORD. We were not allowed to have girlfriends and were required to live a life of integrity. Many in the youth group had girlfriends, so in order not to look bad I lied about having one. Then I got into a real mess because the leadership came to me and said they heard I had a girlfriend. I told them I made it up to make myself look good in front of the guys, but the truth of the matter is at the time they confronted me I did have a girlfriend but denied it.

Lying has been present in my life since I was a child. I was always a people pleaser and wanted to look good in front of others. Pleasing people and always wanting to look good caused an internal battle in my life by telling the truth when I sinned. I would confess I was sinning, but not speak the entire truth, especially in the area of sexual immorality. I would confess to my parents about things I did wrong to another individual. Even if it wasn't that bad, I would admit the fault, but put excuses to it and blame the other person. It was a defense to make myself look good and not look so bad. As a Christian, I struggled with lying for a lot of years. It took a lot for me to realize it was pride. I used to think I was a humble person, and people would tell me all the time that one characteristic they liked about me was my humility, especially on birthday celebrations when people wanted to say nice things to me. This didn't let me see the truth that I had hidden pride and fake humility.

At the beginning of this year HOLY SPIRIT brought such conviction of sin, I had to go to my pastor and confess that when I exposed my sins to him in the past, I was not completely honest and only told him part of the truth. I didn't want him to see how deep my sin was. My conscience kept telling me I had to be totally honest with him. I felt very strongly about that. It got to the point where I felt I would lose my salvation if I didn't confess my lies. I was so afraid, but the conviction of HOLY SPIRIT was stronger than the fear of being rejected. I openly confessed everything, and to my surprise I didn't find rejection. What I received was mercy, grace, and restoration. Because I had a repented heart and renounced pride and lying, the LORD transformed my life. I no longer need to lie to feel accepted, I just need to be honest. The Word of GOD tells us the truth shall set us free and I'm a living testimony of that."

The only way to break your pride is by walking in humility and confessing your sins. Although it may be difficult to admit your faults, with the help of HOLY SPIRIT, you can do it.

What are your intentions?

Have you ever sweet-talked to someone to get your way? This is a form of flattery and it is deceitful because you are speaking to them with the intent of having them do a favor for you.

> They speak idly everyone with his neighbor; with flattering lips and a double heart they speak. May the LORD cut off all flattering lips and the tongue that speaks proud things.
> - Psalms 12:2-3

What are the intentions behind the words you speak? If you are using overpraises or compliments to control another individual or as a form of persuasion you are sinning. You are taking advantage of an individual with your selfish motives.

Do you stretch the truth?

Individuals who exaggerate usually do so because of pride or a lack of self-confidence. Looking good is a powerful motivator to twist a story or to deliberately exaggerate, sometimes at the cost of making others look bad. Merriam-Webster's dictionary defines exaggeration as follows: to enlarge beyond the truth, to enlarge or increase especially beyond the normal.[1] "You never listen to me!" "You always get your way." These statements embellish the truth. Be careful using the words always or never. These are words people often use to overstate the truth and draw attention to themselves. Exaggeration can be in the form of adding details to make the story more interesting or humorous. Some people amplify their illness to gain sympathy and attention from others. If your words are flavored with exaggeration, you are bearing false witness.

What impression are you giving?

Giving false impressions is another subtle way of breaking the ninth commandment. It is an attempt to create a better impression of oneself. In Acts 5 you can read where Ananias and Sapphira sold their possessions and acted as if they gave all their proceeds to the church. The amount of giving was not the issue. It was the attitude of the heart and the impression they were giving. Peter confronted their deception.

> *"...Why have you conceived this thing in your heart? You have not lied to men but to God."*
> *- Acts 5:4*

Have you ever been complimented for something that you did not do or say, and you accepted the compliment? You are giving a false impression that the work was yours. Anytime you use someone else's work and pretend it is yours, you are giving a false impression and stealing credit from another person's work. This is wrong.

Have you ever been thanked by someone for praying for them when you forgot and never presented their need to the Lord? By saying, "You're welcome" you are giving the pretense that you did pray for them. False impressions are a form of lying.

You can give a false impression because you want to fit in and have people accept you. You are afraid if people knew the truth about you, they may not want to associate with you. This was the root of Karen's lying. Here is her testimony.

"I grew up in a home where lying was natural. My mother used to solve her problems by lying. So, to me, lying was a normal way of life. My dad left when I was nine years old and all my friends had their fathers living with them. For me to fit in, I would make up lies about things I supposedly did with my father, that I went somewhere with him, or we did something together, things we never did. I was giving a false impression that I had a wonderful relationship with my father. Lying became a pattern in my life. It was so normal to lie that I created a story and then actually believed that it happened. That would stay with me and I would share it, lying like it was true. Growing up, I used to lie to fill a void that I had in my soul because of the rejection of my father and the lack of a relationship with him. The fantasies I used to tell my friends were my way of coping with the emptiness I felt because my father was not around. I wanted my friends to like me and felt if they knew the truth, they wouldn't accept me.

When I turned fifteen, the Lord began to transform my life and I was baptized with the Holy Spirit. However, there was still a habit that needed to be broken from my life—lying. The Holy Spirit brought conviction of my sin and I realized it was wrong. The lying was so strong, it was a stronghold in my life and at that time I didn't know how to deal with it. It was very hard for me to quit lying and be free from it. Years passed and one day I came to understand that this stronghold of lying was an open door in my life. It was not only a generational curse. It was breaking God's commandment. This was hurting my spiritual life. Lying was pulling me farther away from God. I went through a process of deliverance and the demon of lying was rebuked out of my life and I was set free. The demon was gone, but the habit of lying instilled in my mind had to be broken.

One day I remember the Lord spoke to me to write in a notebook every single verse in the Bible that had to do with lying. That's what I did. I grabbed a notebook and wrote all the verses about lying. When I was reading them, it was such an eye-opener for me. The Word of God washed me, and I understood the spiritual consequences of lying. I understood that lying was a sin and I was offending the heart of the Lord. It was a very beautiful process the Lord did through His Word. As the Word washed me, I started breaking those patterns of lying with the help of Holy Spirit.

In time, I was able to break the habit of lying. But occasionally, I would catch myself slipping. Immediately Holy Spirit brought conviction of my sin and I would go to the individual and tell them "I'm sorry, I just lied to you. I'm in the process of being set free from this and please forgive me." There was so much conviction, I had to stop and correct the lie immediately. Praise God I am no longer tormented with a lying spirit. I've learned that even exaggerating is a lie. Sometimes we think that exaggerating is alright, but it is not. Blessed be the name of the Lord for His Word that confronts our sin, the blood of Jesus that delivers us, and the power of Holy Spirit that gives us the strength to overcome."

When individuals struggle with rejection, it is not unusual for them to use exaggeration or false impressions. It makes them feel better about themselves and they use it to get people to accept them. If you struggle with rejection, uproot that spirit so you no longer use exaggeration or false impressions to cover it up. You will realize that people will accept you for who you are.

What example are you setting?

Children learn from an early age that lying is acceptable through the actions of their parents or other adults. Has someone ever called you and you didn't want to talk to them, so you had your family member tell them you weren't home, even though you were? Have you ever commented to a person and in the privacy of your home speak the opposite? Children often hear their parents speak nicely when face to face with an individual, but once the individual isn't around, speak spiteful things about the person. Many times, we say things, not realizing our children are listening. They sometimes overhear their parents call off work using the excuse of not feeling well, knowing their parents have lied just so they could have the day off for leisurely pleasure. Is it any wonder children don't tell the truth when they are confronted with something they have done wrong? They learned by example.

How many parents, including Christians, have raised their children believing in Santa Claus? Even before HOLY SPIRIT brought conviction that celebrating Christmas was wrong, I never raised my children believing in Santa Claus. You may think the Santa Claus fantasy is just fun and no harm will come from it. Alongside this, you are also training your children up in the things of the LORD. What kind of confusion does it bring when they realize you have fooled them into believing that Santa Claus was real? It can open a door for them to question the reality of JESUS. They may think if Santa Claus isn't real, then maybe JESUS isn't real either!

The best way to teach children integrity is through your actions. Do your actions line up with what you speak? Are you walking and speaking with integrity? Set a good example for your children and those around you?

Have you broken any promises?

One common area of disobeying the ninth commandment is through broken promises. When you make a promise, you are expected to fulfill that promise. Have you ever made a promise to GOD, "GOD if you _____ I promised to _____" and then fall short of your promise? The LORD takes seriously the promises you make to Him. If you have made a promise to the LORD and have not fulfilled it, you have a debt with Him.

GOD also holds you accountable for the promises you make to others. Have you ever made a promise to help someone and then back out of that promise? How many children's hearts have been broken because of broken promises made by their parents? If you are not sure you can keep a promise, it is best not to make them. Keeping promises demonstrates the integrity of your heart.

> "Again, you have heard that it was said to those of old, 'You shall not swear falsely, but shall perform your oaths to the Lord.' But I say to you, do not swear at all: neither by heaven, for it is God's throne; nor by the earth, for it is His footstool; nor by Jerusalem, for it is the city of the great King. Nor shall you swear by your head, because you cannot make one hair white or black. But let your 'Yes' be 'Yes,' and your 'No,' 'No.' For whatever is more than these is from the evil one."
>
> - Matthew 5:33-37

> If a man makes a vow to the LORD or swears an oath to bind himself by some agreement, he shall not break his word; he shall do according to all that proceeds out of his mouth.
> - Numbers 30:2

Some individuals feel uncomfortable praying in front of others but promise to do so in their privacy. Make sure you follow through. When you make a promise to pray for someone, that individual is counting on your prayers to help them through a difficult situation. Many times, you have good intentions, but because of busyness or forgetfulness, you don't follow through with what you promised.

You should not be hasty in making promises. Make sure you can fulfill each commitment you make. Otherwise, you will go against your word and tarnish your integrity.

What kind of witness are you?

When you think of a witness, you usually associate it with the court of law and bringing justice to a crime. A witness is someone who can testify that something is true because they have seen it with their own eyes or heard it with their ears. You can be a false witness by telling an untruth or a partial truth. You can also be a false witness if you see or hear something that needs to be reported and remain silent and doesn't say anything. If you have ever made the appearance as though an individual was innocent, when in fact, they had done something wrong, you are giving a misperception.

Has someone ever come to you and said something about another individual and you go and tell someone else what you heard? That is gossip and you could be slandering another individual. If you did not see the event or hear it firsthand, how do you know what you are spreading is the truth? You could be speaking falsely and ruining someone's reputation. What is the motive behind you telling another individual? When you spread false reports about an individual, you are bearing false witness and slandering their reputation.

How do you judge?

Have you ever prejudged someone without having all the facts? So often people are quick to judge others. You must make every effort to thoroughly seek the facts before making any judgment of wrongdoing. Your standard for judging needs to be determined by God's Word. You should present the Word of God in love to someone who is sinning. Have them read the scripture aloud and let Holy Spirit bring the conviction of sin.

"Do not judge according to appearance, but judge with righteous judgment."

- John 7:24

I know of individuals who have left a church because the church's leadership had confronted sin and reprimanded them for it. Rather than repenting and correcting their behavior, some leave out of rebellion and say things that are not true against the pastor or others in leadership. Individuals who resist biblical authority are proud people who are eager to falsely accuse a man or woman of GOD. Satan loves it when he can find individuals who are willing to speak evil about pastors and church members. He will use these false accusations to harm pastors and their ministries. We are to protect the reputation of other believers, not divide the body of Christ.

Are you part of the solution?

If we are honest with each other, many of us would admit we have spoken badly about another individual. Why is it that people love to talk about others, especially when it is something bad? Gossip spreads like wildfire. If you listen to the gossip, you are just as guilty as the one speaking. Some will use praying as a cover-up for gossip. "Did you hear about so and so?" After giving every detail of the situation, they then say, "Pray for them." Don't fall into the snare. Take the petition before GOD yourself.

Where there is no wood, the fire goes out; And where there is no talebearer, strife ceases.

- Proverbs 26:20

Rather than being part of the problem, be part of the solution? There is a Biblical protocol in Matthew 18:15 that must be followed when you are speaking badly about another individual. I wonder if the gossiper would say those things to you if the other individual was standing there with you? Probably not. How can you be part of the solution? Rather than standing there and listening, tell the individual you are not interested in listening to idle talk and walk away. Another way is to say to the gossiper, "Oh, you have something to say about _____, let me put him/her on the phone so they can hear what you are saying about them.

> He who goes about as a talebearer reveals secrets; Therefore,
> do not associate with one who flatters with his lips.
> *- Proverbs 20:19*

You cannot fall into the snare of gossiping. Flee from it and from those who love to entertain it. Don't add to the fire, quench it! Speak blessing to one another rather than curses.

Who told you?

With people searching for answers for their lives, it could be very easy to think GOD is speaking to us when He is not. When you say, "GOD told me _____", be sure it was from GOD and not from your emotions, wishful thinking, or even from the enemy. People sometimes release a word and say "Thus says the LORD" when GOD never spoke to them in the first place. If you use the prophetic to manipulate or dominate another person in the name of the LORD, you are profaning His name. When you falsely say something is from GOD, and it is not, you are using GOD's name in vain and bearing false witness.

> And the LORD said to me, "The prophets prophesy lies in My name. I have not sent them, commanded them, nor spoken to them; they prophesy to you a false vision, divination, a worthless thing, and the deceit of their heart."
> *- Jeremiah 14:14*

Any time you receive a prophetic word, pray about it, share it with your spiritual leaders, and wait for confirmation. If you run after a word that did not originate from GOD, you could be falling into a trap of the enemy. GOD will always confirm His Word.

What Web Are You Making?

Does your life portray the reputation as one who is true to his or her words? One day you will have to give an account to every word that has proceeded out of your mouth.

Questions for Thought
1. What does it mean to be a false witness?
2. What are the ways you can become a false witness?
3. How can not saying something be just as bad as lying?
4. What is the Biblical protocol to follow when someone has offended you?
5. What is the righteous way of judging?

Are you walking with integrity? Get rid of the old nature and strive to be a godly witness for JESUS. Refer to Section 3, Ninth Commandment to continue your process of deliverance.

Chapter 17
WHAT DO YOU LONG FOR?

Commandment Ten
*"You shall not covet your neighbor's house; you shall not
covet your neighbor's wife, nor his male servant, nor his
female servant, nor his ox, nor his donkey, nor anything that
is your neighbor's."*
- Exodus 20:17

The tenth commandment instructs us not to covet what others have. It is GOD's way of protecting you from greed and protecting others of their possessions. To understand this commandment, you must understand what the word covet means. According to the Merriam-Webster's Dictionary to covet means to wish for earnestly, to extremely desire what belongs to another.[1] Strong's Concordance defines the Hebrew root word as to greatly delight in beauty, to covet, to lust.[2] In other words, covetousness is having an intense craving or desire for something that does not belong to you. When you allow greed, lust, and envy to be the motivators of your actions, you are breaking the tenth commandment. It should be GOD who motivates your actions. Anything else is idolatry.

For this you know that no fornicator, unclean person, nor covetous man, who is an idolater, has any inheritance in the kingdom of Christ and God.

- Ephesians 5:5

The Word of GOD tells us a covetous man is an idolater and if your heart is full of covetousness, you will not inherit eternal life. This commandment brings to full circle the sin of idolatry. It forbids it in the first commandment and again confronting it in the last commandment. Because of your self-centeredness, you seek after your desire regardless of how it will affect others or how it will affect your relationship with GOD. Your desires become your god. Coveting is telling yourself I must have it no matter what!

Covetousness has been a downfall for man since the beginning of time and we see it throughout the Bible. Adam and Eve coveted the forbidden fruit, took of it, ate it, and disobeyed GOD. We read in the last chapter how Achan coveted the silver and gold, which caused him and his family their lives (Joshua 7:20-21). It was covetousness over Uriah's wife Bathsheba which caused King David to commit adultery, and then plot his murder to cover up his sin (2 Samuel 11). It was Ahab's covetousness for Naboth's vineyard that caused Jezebel to bear a false report against Naboth and had him stoned so her husband could receive the vineyard he so desired (1 Kings 21:9-10). Judas coveted and sold JESUS for thirty pieces of silver. Coveting continues to be a downfall for people today.

Why is covetousness a dangerous sin?

If you struggle with covetousness, it opens the door to break every other commandment. When the Pharisees tested JESUS and asked Him which is the great commandment in the law, He answered:

> *Jesus said to him, "You shall love the LORD your God with all your heart, with all your soul, and with all your mind. This is the first and great commandment. And the second is like it: You shall love your neighbor as yourself."*
> *- Matthew 22:37-39*

You cannot love the LORD with all your heart, soul, and mind if you are coveting something or someone. Your priority is no longer on the things of GOD. Your heart and mind are focused on earthly things. When you place something or someone before GOD, you have committed spiritual adultery and have broken this first and great commandment. As mentioned earlier, idolatry has entered your heart. Referring to Matthew 22, loving your neighbor is the second greatest commandment. If you love your neighbor, you won't murder nor commit adultery against them. If you love your neighbor, you will not steal from them, nor will you bear false witness against them. Yet, this is exactly what happens when covetousness enters your heart. Individuals will murder, commit adultery, lie, and/or steal to obtain that person, place, or possession they are obsessed with.

Who do you serve?

When you covet the things of this world, you devote your time, finances, and energy to achieving them. Before you know it, they begin to govern your life, which is contrary to the Word of GOD. Your covetousness soon takes priority and becomes your focus. The LORD is the One who should be the center of your life.

> *"No one can serve two masters; for either he will hate the one and love the other, or else he will be loyal to the one and despise the other. You cannot serve God and mammon."*
> - *Matthew 6:24*

From the scripture above, you can see how covetousness and idolatry complement each other. The spirit of mammon entices you to seek after wealth for your present enjoyment. Covetousness causes you to spend way beyond your income and living beyond your financial boundaries. Your focus in life now centers around how you are going to make ends meet and pay your bills. Many people exhaust themselves working overtime just to meet their budgets. Proverbs 22:7 tells us that the borrower is servant to the lender. Your debt now has control of your life and your money. Every time you pay interest, you become a slave to the lender. If you are in debt over your head, search your heart. You are to be a servant of GOD and not subject yourself to a lender who charges high interest.

GOD's Word tells us to seek first the Kingdom of GOD. Your primary goal should not be to seek financial prosperity or possessions but to help those who are less fortunate than you. This is the total opposite of the way society thinks. Your desire for prosperity should be so you can bless others. You are not to live a self-centered life. You are called to love your neighbors, especially those less fortunate than you. You are called to give generously the wealth and talents you have been blessed with so you can be a blessing to others. By doing so, you are investing in the Kingdom of GOD. What is your heart's desire, is it on earthly possessions or treasures in Heaven?

How is your contentment?

Have you ever caught yourself saying things like "I just got to have this" or "That was supposed to be mine"? When you say or think these things, you are not demonstrating an attitude of appreciation for what the LORD has already blessed you with.

> *Let your conduct be without covetousness; be content with such things as you have.*
> *- Hebrews 13:5*

Covetousness is the opposite of contentment. Contentment means being satisfied with what you have and realizing GOD has given you everything you need. Nowadays, because you live in a society of instant gratification, you quickly fulfill the desires of your flesh without seriously considering its ramification. You may have a perfectly working cell phone or iPad, but because a newer version promises to be quicker or offers better features, you buy it on credit. If you see something you want, you just pull out the credit card from your wallet and use it. Before you know it, you are in a downward spiral of endless debt. Some debts never seem to get paid off because you keep buying more things out of greed and not out of necessity. If this sounds like you, you are covetous.

I know of an individual in his late twenties who wanted one of the latest electronic games. His wife told him they could not afford it right now and he would have to wait. He pouted for three weeks, not talking to her until she gave in and allowed him to buy "his toy". This behavior is childish, self-centered, and displeasing to the LORD.

Contentment should not depend on material possessions. Some individuals go shopping every time they feel depressed, thinking this will make them feel better. They quickly discover that what they thought would bring joy and lasting fulfillment brought disappointments, temporary pleasure, and an added expense to their budget. If you are looking for contentment in your life, seek after GOD. He will supply all that you ever need.

> *"But seek first the kingdom of God and His righteousness, and all these things shall be added to you."*
>
> - *Matthew 6:33*

Is wishful thinking wrong?

I'm sure you have seen something at one time or another and have said, "I wish I could buy that", or "man I would love to have that". Where do you draw the line regarding wishing for something and coveting? When you have a wish list, you wait upon the LORD to open the door for you to obtain that item. You put it in His hands and let it go. You trust that if GOD wants us to have it, one day it will be yours. However, coveting goes much deeper than just wishing for something. It preoccupies your thoughts and fills your heart with intense desires. Coveting causes you to have envy when you see someone that has something that you want. Rather than being happy for the individual, you become jealous and envious, saying things like, "He doesn't deserve that" or "I should have been the one to get the promotion". If you struggle with this type of attitude and cannot rejoice when someone else prospers, you are breaking the tenth commandment. Be careful! Resentment and hatred can settle in your heart. You may even go as far as to wish you were in someone else's shoes. Here is a testimony of Heather who realized the covetous trap the enemy was plotting for her life.

"We have been programmed by this world to desire more...bigger...better. Every day we admire things and situations. It seems harmless to simply glance into a store and desire the outfits perfectly set before us. We call it "window shopping". Unknowingly that pattern of looking and wanting begins to creep into every aspect of our life. Thoughts begin to take root. As we fix on some of the seemingly attractive things around us, we start to hunger for what we see. A glance at a couple in the church who are equally yoked and committed to the LORD can set your heart to gazing at other marriages. Soon you find yourself yearning for something that appears out of your reach, and you question the relationship you've been in for 38 years because it lacks the intimacy and oneness you notice elsewhere. The enemy, Satan, seeks to rob, steal, and destroy. He looks for open doors where he can gain access. He sees our heart's desires and enters, prepared to reap havoc.

The Word of GOD tells us to give thanks in everything! When we fall prey to a "window shopping" mentality, we violate the tenth commandment...DO NOT COVET. While "admiring" seems like an acceptable pastime, our adversary is waiting to pounce. He slowly lures you with delectable morsels, then suddenly you find yourself trapped in his snare. Your happiness waivers and discontent emerge.

Fortunately, we have someone we can call upon to rescue us. The moment we recognize our sin and repent, JESUS can free us from the snare. I am grateful for the mercy of our LORD who opened my eyes to see that secretly I was coveting godly marriages. He showed me that while I was admiring other relationships, I was tearing a hole in mine. A covetous spirit is a breeding ground for spirits of jealousy, envy, and discontent. Once he knows you're listening, Satan is eager to plant every seed that you allow to grow.

That covetous spirit almost cost me my marriage, but at the mercy of the LORD, He revealed the open door that gave the enemy a foothold in my marriage. It is painful to confess that I had reached a point where I believed GOD wanted me to separate from my husband. Fortunately, a wise leader advised me to wait until the end of the Counting of the Omer. This is fifty days where you cry out to the LORD to search your heart and show you any wickedness that you are entertaining. It was during this time the LORD graciously opened my eyes. After repenting of my sin, He cleansed my heart and thoughts and humbled me to understand the changes I needed to make to transform my marriage. Ouch!!!

The first step required putting GOD first, then treating my husband with equal respect. This is an ongoing process, but I am forever grateful for the awakening that occurred when GOD led me to repent of comparing my marriage to others. Did Satan just vanish? Oh No! He switched gears and started working on my husband. One day I was shocked and crushed when my husband disclosed a desire to separate. Fortunately, I was also wiser in discerning the enemy's tactics. This time I cried out, determined the enemy was not taking what's mine.

We are growing and gaining understanding. We may not be perfectly yoked yet, but I am truly blessed by my husband. When the 2020 pandemic clears, I am praying we can renew our vows and eat from a celebratory cake to honor the LORD and His unending grace."

From the testimony above you can see the dangers of coveting. You get your eyes off what GOD has blessed you with and set them on things that GOD never intended you to have. Praise GOD for the victory in Heather's life!

Could you pass the test?

The LORD has a way of testing our hearts. In Matthew 19, the rich young ruler asked JESUS what he could do to inherit eternal life. JESUS told him to go sell what he had and give to the poor. The young man went away sorrowful because he had great possessions. His emotional attachment to his wealth superseded his willingness to follow JESUS. His covetousness and greed prevented him from being a blessing to others and storing up treasures in heaven.

A few years ago, my husband and I were saving money to buy a new home. We had a nice amount saved and were excited at the possibility of moving out of our townhouse and into a home that had a back porch and a nice back yard to enjoy. One Sunday we had a guest speaker preaching and the LORD prompted him to release a prophetic word that our church was to have its building. He asked the congregation to come to present an I-O-U note to the LORD for a designated amount of money and initiated the building fund. GOD was testing our hearts to see how we would respond. Were we going to covet the new home we were desiring or give what was asked of us for the house of the LORD? HOLY SPIRIT deposited in our hearts the amount to give, we came into agreement and gave with a cheerful heart. To this day we are still living in the townhouse, hoping to have it paid off in five years. One day, the LORD may open the door for us to buy a home with a nice piece of property. Until then, we are very content living in the home He has blessed us with.

What if you were given a promotion and the LORD told you not to take it because He had someone else in mind for the job. Would you be able to give it up? This happened to our pastor years ago when working for a rescue mission center. GOD showed him that a coworker was in a much bigger need than he was for the job. He obeyed and both were blessed. You may be asking, "If the LORD wanted the other individual to get the promotion, why wasn't he offered the promotion first?" GOD was testing the heart of my pastor. Had he been greedy, his attitude would have been, "No way, I've worked hard to get that promotion and I'm not giving it up." Instead, he moved with compassion and cared about his coworker's greater need than his own need.

I remember a couple sharing an experience they had with the LORD. They bought a brand-new refrigerator. Before getting rid of their older one, they heard about an individual in desperate need of a refrigerator. They were about to give the lady the used refrigerator, but GOD spoke to them and told them they needed to give her the brand-new one. Both felt they had heard correctly from the LORD and chose to obey. This individual could not believe strangers would give her a brand-new refrigerator. GOD's love for this lady was demonstrated through this couple. Praise GOD for their obedience.

Where is your focus?

There is a false gospel being preached that is based upon covetousness. The prosperity gospel places too much value on earthly blessings and does little to confront sin. It fosters a mindset where its followers see GOD as an ATM and entice people with a promise of a life of wealth. Many honest and sincere preachers start with good intentions, only to be led astray by greed. They look at the size of their congregation and the building they worship in as a measuring rod for their success. Their focus turns away from the souls to the size of their congregation.

> *But those who desire to be rich fall into temptation and a snare, and into many foolish and harmful lusts which drown men in destruction and perdition. For the love of money is a root of all kinds of evil, for which some have strayed from the faith in their greediness and pierced themselves through with many sorrows.*
> *- 1 Timothy 6:9-10*

I once went to a conference in Orlando to hear a well-known evangelist. On the first night during the offering, he announced anyone who gave $1,000 would be allowed on stage and he would personally pray for them. This is unbiblical and distorts the gospel because it is putting a price on prayer. Just because someone has $1000 to give, are they more deserving of prayer than those who cannot give? This type of treatment is giving preference to one person over another and the book of James warns us against that.

> My brethren do not hold the faith of our Lord Jesus Christ, the Lord of glory, with partiality. For if there should come into your assembly a man with gold rings, in fine apparel, and there should also come in a poor man in filthy clothes, and you pay attention to the one wearing the fine clothes and say to him, "You sit here in a good place," and say to the poor man, "You stand there," or, "Sit here at my footstool," have you not shown partiality among yourselves, and become judges with evil thoughts?
>
> *- James 2:1-4*

No one should ever put a price on praying for someone. I was in shock when I heard this evangelist announce that. I immediately stood up and walked out of that conference and never returned.

> By covetousness they will exploit you with deceptive words; for a long time, their judgment has not been idle, and their destruction does not slumber.
>
> *- 2 Peter 2:3*

Prosperity preachers will prey on the poor and elderly with their "hundredfold" snare. They lure their listeners into giving hundreds or thousands of dollars believing they are planting a seed of faith that will grow into a harvest of a hundredfold. This is manipulation, twisting of the Word of GOD, and is sinful. If the LORD wants you to give a large sum of money to a ministry, He will place it upon your heart even without the ministry asking for an offering. Always seek the LORD in prayer before sowing into a ministry other than your local church.

Where is your focus? Do you see other servants of the LORD prosperous and wish you were like them? Do you question why GOD is blessing one ministry and not your own? You may see a very successful ministry, but you don't know what it took to get them there. You don't know the trials and tribulations that brought success. GOD rarely blesses with instant success because it opens the door to pride. Don't despise your small beginnings? Don't envy what you don't have. GOD is at work. He is growing and maturing you, building His characteristics in you to prepare you for what's to come. Enjoy the blessings of godliness and contentment.

Questions for Thought
1. What does covet mean?
2. How does GOD see individuals with covetousness? (Ephesians 5:5)
3. Why is it difficult for a rich person to become a disciple of JESUS? (Matthew 6:24)
4. What is the opposite of covetousness?
5. When does prosperity become a sin?

Are you spending frivolously and seeking contentment in the wrong places? Refer to Section 3, Tenth Commandment to continue your process of deliverance.

SECTION 3

MINISTERING DELIVERANCE

Chapter 18
FIRST COMMANDMENT

Remember that sin opens the door for demonic influences in your life. I trust you have already received JESUS as your Savior. If not, this is needed before your deliverance process. It will change your life forever. Here is a simple prayer to begin your relationship with the LORD.

Heavenly FATHER,

I recognize that I am a sinner and I ask forgiveness for my sins. I want to turn my life around. Thank you for sending your Son who died on the cross for my sins. JESUS, cleanse me of all my sins and become LORD of my life. Deliver me from every stronghold in my life that hinders me from following Your commandments. I ask You HOLY SPIRIT to guide me in all paths of truth and help me to follow GOD's plan for my life. In JESUS's name, I pray. Amen!

If you have not done so, take time to pray and fast before your deliverance. Do not rush into this. Seek HOLY SPIRIT to guide you in this process.

The following is a list of activities that are forbidden according to the first commandment. If you have engaged in any of these, you have violated the first commandment and exposed yourself to demonic influences. Close these doors so the enemy cannot bring an accusation against you. The spirit attached to these activities needs to be bound and rebuked. Take time to reflect and ask HOLY SPIRIT to bring to memory those things you or your ancestors have done to break the first commandment. Identify the ones that that apply to you.

- Any religion that denies JESUS as the Son of the Living GOD
- Astral projection
- Astrology (Horoscope reading)
- Brazilian Jiu-Jitsu
- Clairvoyance (seeing mental images through psychic abilities)
- Divination
- Drugs (If you are under the influence of drugs or alcohol Satan will take advantage of your passive state of mind.
- Enchantment
- Extra sensorial perception (ESP), telepathy
- Eye Reading
- Freemasonry or any other secret society
- Good luck charms
- Hard rock music (any music with violence & hatred)
- Occult books/movies/ video games
- Hypnosis
- Kundalini
- Levitation
- Magic
- Martial arts (Karate, Taekwondo, Kung Fu, Judo, Kendo)
- Meditation (through Yoga)
- Mind control
- Mind reading
- New Age Movement
- New Era
- Ouija board and other occult games
- Practicing or seeking after warlocks, witches, sorcerers, psychics
- Reiki (healing through universal energy)

- Santeria
- Saturnalia (spirit behind celebrating Christmas)
- Séances (necromancy, invoking spirits of the dead)
- Spirit Guides
- Superstitions
- Telekinesis (power to move things)
- Transcendental Meditation
- Voodoo
- White magic
- Witchcraft of any form (Including tarot cards, crystal ball, tea leaves, palm reading, egg passing, fortunetelling, handwriting analysis)

Ask HOLY SPIRIT to reveal any other open doors that may not be included in this list. Journal everything HOLY SPIRIT reveals to you.

_____
_____
_____
_____

Once you have written your thoughts down, the first step is to confess your sins and repent by asking forgiveness. I have included a prayer guide. It is only a guide. Seek HOLY SPIRIT to help you in this process. He knows where you have been and what you have done. Pray as HOLY SPIRIT guides you.

Heavenly FATHER,

I ask forgiveness for every sin I have committed. Forgive me of any past or present involvement in the occult. I ask forgiveness for every form of witchcraft, magic, sorcery, or divination I have opened myself up to. I repent of them now in the name of JESUS.

I ask forgiveness for the sins of my ancestors who have transgressed against your first commandment. I ask forgiveness for any rebellion I have in my heart. I recognize I have disobeyed Your Word and have sought after supernatural experiences apart from You. I ask forgiveness for breaking Your first commandment. (Begin asking forgiveness for specific sins that HOLY SPIRIT reveals to you.) I ask forgiveness for celebrating pagan holidays (name each of them) and not celebrating your feasts. I ask forgiveness for eating foods dedicated to these pagan holidays. I know it is only through the blood of JESUS that I can be set free. In JESUS's name, I pray.

I renounce every demonic stronghold that keeps me from obeying Your first commandment and I call upon You LORD JESUS to set me free. I renounce every cult and philosophy that denies the deity of JESUS. In the name of JESUS, I renounce every psychic and occult practice that I have been involved in knowingly or unknowingly (name each one). Refer to the list of activities you have circled above. I renounce any spirit I opened myself to through celebrating pagan holidays. I renounce the addiction to sugar that entered through the eating of candy associated with pagan holidays.

Begin binding and rebuking any spirit from your life that HOLY SPIRIT reveals to you. When you bind a spirit, you are restricting its power. Here are some examples: the spirit of magic, the spirit of divination, the spirit of death, demons that entered through witchcraft, the spirit of violence, the spirit of Pharmacia, the spirit of necromancy, the spirit of Santeria, etc. I bind every spirit that entered through _____ and I order it out of my life. I bind the spirit of _____ and rebuke it out of my life. (Begin naming them one by one.) I order it out, never to return in the name of JESUS. (Repeat this with every spirit that has you bound.)

I go back four generations and in the name of JESUS, I break the power of any curse off myself and my generations because of witchcraft or sorcery coming from my ancestors in JESUS's name. I break all curses of physical or mental sickness or disease. I cancel the curse of death off my life and my generations in JESUS's name. I close every door I have opened through the breaking of the first commandment. Satan, I break your powers off my life, off my children, my grandchildren, and my great-grandchildren in the name of JESUS.

HOLY SPIRIT, come and fill my life with your presence. Guide me in all truth. I want to walk in righteousness and receive the blessings you have for my life. In JESUS's name, I pray. Amen!

There is one last step that must be taken to receive the ultimate freedom. You don't want to leave any open doors for Satan to claim legal rights.

Are you ready for some spring cleaning?

Clean your home from all items such as paraphernalia books, videos, games, good luck charms, and music related to witchcraft, magic, or violence.

> *Also, many of those who had practiced magic brought their books together and burned them in the sight of all.*
> *– Acts 19:19*

Ask HOLY SPIRIT to guide you as you go through your house. Destroy anything that has to do with false religions. If you have any relics or souvenirs from foreign countries, ask HOLY SPIRIT if there are demonic spirits associated with them. Destroy all decorations used to decorate and celebrate pagan holidays. Do not place these items in a garage sale or give them to some other individual. In doing so you are enabling others to celebrate pagan holidays.

As the last prayer rededicate your home to the LORD, invite HOLY SPIRIT to habitat with you. Take responsibility for maintaining your deliverance. That can only be done if you maintain a life of praying, reading the Word of GOD, building an intimate relationship with HOLY SPIRIT and allowing Him to take control of every area of your life.

Once you have finished praying ask the LORD if there is anything else you need to do to restore His heart.

Return to Section 2 and begin reading *Chapter 09 - What is Your Passion?*

Chapter 19
SECOND COMMANDMENT

The following is a list of questions that will help determine if you have violated the second commandment. Identify the ones that apply to you.

- Have you bowed down to any carved image? (This includes kneeling to any statue)
- Have you worshipped any carved image? (Such as the Virgin Mary)
- Have you prayed to any carved image? (Such as a saint)
- Have you built an altar made with carved images? (Put up statues in your home or yard)
- Have you offered incense or burnt candles to any carved image?
- Were you named after any saint or pagan god or goddess?
- Do you worship angels?
- Can you part with your Christmas tree?
- Do you have souvenirs that have been dedicated to Satan?
- Have you committed spiritual adultery by turning your back on GOD?
- Are you stubborn and set in your ways?
- Are you prideful and consider you know better than GOD what's best for your life?
- Is your job or career your priority?

- Are you obsessed with making money or gaining material things?
- Does your life center on pleasing your spouse rather than pleasing GOD?
- Have you placed your children/spouse/possessions above the LORD?
- Have you placed your ministry above the LORD?

Take time to reflect and ask the LORD to bring to memory those things you have done to offend Him through breaking the second commandment. Journal below.

_____

_____

_____

Once you have written your thoughts, confess your sins, and ask forgiveness. I have included a prayer guide.

Heavenly FATHER,

I ask forgiveness for breaking Your second commandment. I ask forgiveness for my stubbornness, self-centeredness, rebellion, and my pride. I ask forgiveness for every form of idolatry in my life. (Begin asking forgiveness for specific sins that HOLY SPIRIT reveals to you.) I recognize I have opened doors through my disobedience to allow demonic influences in my life. I know it is only through the blood of JESUS that I can be set free. In JESUS's name, I pray, Amen.

The following is a list of spirits/demons associated with the sins listed above. It does not mean you are demon-possessed, but these demonic forces may have you bound and affect your relationship with GOD. Circle all that pertains to you. There may be other spirits as well. Ask HOLY SPIRIT to reveal any that may not be listed.

- Spirit of idolatry
- Spiritual adultery

- Spirit of error
- Spirit of rebellion
- Spirit of stubbornness
- Spirit of pride
- Spirit of self-centeredness
- Spirit of selfishness
- Spirit of mammon
- Spirit of addiction
- Spirit of fantasy
- Spirit of death
- Spirit of oppression

Heavenly FATHER,

I renounce every demonic stronghold that stops me from obeying Your second commandment. I renounce my rebellion, stubbornness, self-centeredness, and pride in the name of JESUS. I cancel any right the enemy has over my life because of these open doors in JESUS's name. I renounce every form of idolatry that I or my ancestors have been involved in knowingly and unknowingly. I renounce the spirit of _____ (name each one). Refer to your notes and renounce anything else HOLY SPIRIT may have revealed to you.

I bind the spirit of _____ and rebuke it out of my life. I order it out, never to return in the name of JESUS. (Repeat this with every spirit that has you bound.)

I go back four generations and in the name of JESUS, I break the power of any curse off myself and my generations because of the idolatry of my ancestors in JESUS's name. I close every door I have opened through the breaking of the second commandment. Satan, I break your powers off my life, off my children, my grandchildren, and my great-grandchildren in JESUS's name.

LORD, I put my trust in You. I want you to be first in my life. I choose to submit to Your ways. Fill me with a spirit of humility. Help me to keep my eyes focused on You. Give me the understanding and revelation of celebrating your feasts, in JESUS's name I pray. Amen!

Another step in your process of deliverance is to destroy any images and statues that cause you to break the second commandment. You were asked to destroy all decorations used to decorate and celebrate pagan holidays in the last chapter. I trust you have done so. Dismantle any altars you have made. Throw out all jewelry that would try to imitate the likeness of JESUS or the crucifix. You may have souvenirs or relics dedicated to Satan in your home that you are unaware of. Ask HOLY SPIRIT to show you if you have anything you may have brought into the home that has given Satan a legal right to torment you.

Once you have finished praying, ask the LORD if there is anything you need to do to restore His heart.

Return to Section 2 and begin reading *Chapter 10 – Are You Guilty?*

Chapter 20
THIRD COMMANDMENT

The following questions will help you determine if you have violated the third commandment. Identify the ones that apply to you.

- Have you used GOD's name or the name of JESUS in anger?
- Have you used GOD's name or the name of JESUS in combination with profanity?
- Have you used GOD's name or the name of JESUS carelessly?
- Have you taken an oath in GOD's name or the name of JESUS and falsely spoken?
- Are you professing to be a Christian but not living a Christ-like way?

Take time to reflect and ask HOLY SPIRIT to bring to memory things you have said or done, causing you to break the third commandment.

_____

_____

_____

Heavenly FATHER,
I ask forgiveness for breaking Your third commandment and taking your name in vain. I ask forgiveness for using your name in anger or in ways that did not bring you honor. I ask

forgiveness for not acting Christ-like in my daily walk, for offending you and others because of my testimony. If I have mocked you in any way, I ask your forgiveness. I want to give you the honor you deserve. I know it is only through the blood of JESUS that I can be set free. In JESUS's name, I pray, Amen.

The following is a list of spirits/demons that may be in operation, hindering you from honoring GOD's name. Circle all that pertains to you. There may be other spirits as well, ask HOLY SPIRIT to reveal any that may not be listed.

- Spirit of anger
- Spirit of profanity
- Spirit of vulgarity
- Spirit of hypocrisy
- Spirit of double-mindedness
- Spirit of mockery
- Spirit of defamation
- Spirit of disrespect

Heavenly FATHER

I renounce every demonic stronghold that would cause me to dishonor your name and stop me from obeying Your third commandment. I renounce every form of mockery or dishonor of Your name that I or my ancestors have been involved in knowingly and unknowingly. I renounce the spirit of _____ (name each one separately).

I bind the spirit of _____ and rebuke it out of my life. I order it out, never to return in the name of JESUS. (Repeat this with every spirit that has you bound.)

I go back four generations and in the name of JESUS, I break the power of any curse off myself and my generations because of my ancestors dishonoring Your name. I close every door I have opened through the breaking of the third commandment. Satan, I break your powers off my life, off my children, my grandchildren, and my great-grandchildren in the name of JESUS.

Lord, fill me with Your holiness. May my words be pure and constantly praising You. Fill me with the fruit of Your Spirit so my life will reflect the character of Jesus. I ask these things in Jesus's name. Amen!

Once you have finished praying ask the Lord to show if there is anything else you need to do to restore His heart.

Return to Section 2 and begin reading *Chapter 11 – Have Your Taken Your Break?*

Chapter 21
FOURTH COMMANDMENT

The following is a list of questions that will help determine if you have violated the fourth commandment. Identify the ones that apply to you.

- Are you a workaholic?
- Do you see the Sabbath as a day to catch up on your chores?
- Is your Sabbath packed with activities and little, if any time, seeking rest in God's presence?
- Are you finding that observing the Sabbath is a burden rather than a delight?
- Do you choose to work overtime rather than resting on the Sabbath?
- Are you responsible for others working on the Sabbath?
- Do you choose to spend time on the computer, play video games, or other leisurely activities rather than seeking the Lord on the Sabbath?
- Do your leisure activities stop you from ministering to those in need?
- Are you taking advantage of the welfare system?
- Are you giving 100% when at work?
- Do you take advantage of your parents by paying no rent, nor seeking a job?

Take time to reflect and ask the LORD to bring to memory those things you have done to offend Him through breaking the fourth commandment. Take time to journal your thoughts.

_____

_____

_____

Heavenly FATHER,

I ask forgiveness for not taking seriously the Sabbath and breaking Your fourth commandment. I ask forgiveness for not giving my body the rest that it needs. I ask forgiveness for _____. (Begin asking forgiveness for specific sins that HOLY SPIRIT reveals to you.) I ask forgiveness for allowing anxiety, fear, and worry to rob me of my rest. I know it is only through the blood of JESUS that I can be set free from those things that hold me back from honoring the Sabbath. In JESUS's name, I pray. Amen!

The following is a list of spirits that may be in operation, hindering you from celebrating the Sabbath. Circle all that pertains to you. There may be other spirits as well, ask HOLY SPIRIT to reveal any that may not be listed.

- Spirit of idolatry (to work)
- Spirit of mammon
- Spirit of slavery
- Spirit of busyness
- Spirit of complaining
- Spirit of worry
- Spirit of anxiousness
- Spirit of fear
- Spirit of legalism

Heavenly FATHER,

Thank you for creating the Sabbath for me. I recognize it is important for my physical, emotional, mental, and spiritual well-being. I renounce every mindset that stops me from understanding the importance of the Sabbath in the name of JESUS. I renounce every demonic stronghold that holds me back from obeying Your fourth commandment and I call upon You LORD JESUS to set me free. I renounce the spirit of _____. (Name each one separately.)

I bind and rebuke the spirit of _____ (name each one separately). I order it out of my life, never to return in the name of JESUS.

I go back four generations and in the name of JESUS, I break the power of any curse off myself and my generations because of my ancestors dishonoring the Sabbath.

I close every door I have opened through the breaking of the fourth commandment. Satan, I break your powers off my life, off my children, my grandchildren, and my great-grandchildren in JESUS's name.

LORD, thank you for your mercies over my life. Fill me with Your peace as I put my trust in You. Remove every distraction and help me to rest in Your presence. As I rest in your presence, renew my body, mind, and spirit. In JESUS's name. Amen!

Prayer for Those with Poor Work Ethics

Heavenly FATHER,

Your Word commands us to work. I ask forgiveness for my poor work ethic and for not setting an example for my coworkers. I ask forgiveness for _____. (Begin asking forgiveness for specific sins that HOLY SPIRIT reveals to you.) In JESUS's name, I pray. Amen!

Prayer for Those Who Choose Not to Work

Heavenly FATHER,

I ask forgiveness for my laziness and lack of willingness to find a job. I recognize that I am breaking Your fourth commandment. I ask forgiveness for taking advantage of living freely in my parents' home when I should be contributed to my living expenses. I ask forgiveness for _____. (Begin asking forgiveness for specific sins that HOLY SPIRIT reveals to you.) In JESUS's name, I pray. Amen!

The following is a list of spirits that may be in operation causing poor work ethics. Circle all that pertains to you. There may be other spirits as well, ask HOLY SPIRIT to reveal any that may not be listed.

- Spirit of complacency
- Spirit of procrastination
- Spirit of complaining
- Spirit of laziness

Heavenly FATHER,

I recognize that I have poor work ethics, and this is contrary to your Word. I renounce every demonic stronghold that holds me back from finding/keeping a job. I renounce the spirit of _____. (Name each one.)

I bind the spirit of _____ and rebuke it out of my life. I order it out, never to return in the name of JESUS. (Repeat this with every spirit that has you bound.)

I go back four generations and in the name of JESUS, I break the power of any curse off myself and my generations because of any laziness in my ancestral line.

I close every door I have opened through the breaking of the fourth commandment. Satan, I break your powers off my life, off my children, my grandchildren, and my great-grandchildren in the name of JESUS.

LORD, show me the job that You have for my life. Help me develop good work ethics, that could bring glory and honor to You. In JESUS's name, I pray, Amen!

Once you have finished praying ask the LORD to show if there is anything you need to do to restore His heart.

Return to Section 2 and begin reading *Chapter 12 – How Can I With So Much Pain.*

Chapter 22
FIFTH COMMANDMENT

The following is a list of questions that will help determine if you have violated the fifth commandment. Identify the ones that apply to you.

To young children/teenagers:
- Do you hold unforgiveness, resentment, bitterness, or other negative emotion towards your father or mother?
- Do you talk back to your father or mother?
- Are you disrespectful to your father or mother?
- Do you disobey your father or mother?
- Have you gossiped or criticized your father or mother to others to bring shame?
- Are you ungrateful for what your father or mother has done for you?
- Have your gestures or body language brought dishonor to your father or mother?
- Have you physically hit your father or mother?
- Have you verbally abused your father or mother?
- Have you mocked your father or mother?
- Have you cursed your father or mother?
- Have you lied to your father or mother?
- Have you spoken sarcastically to your father or mother?
- Have you insulted your father or mother?
- Have you ever stolen from your father or mother?

To adult children:

- Do you hold a grudge against your father or mother?
- Do you hold any lack of forgiveness, resentment, bitterness, or other negative emotion towards your father or mother?
- Have you neglected to physically care for your father or mother?
- Have you physically abused your father or mother? (hitting, pushing, depriving them of personal care)
- Have you verbally abused your father or mother? (yelling, humiliation, ridicule, intimidation)
- Have you gossiped or criticized your father or mother to bring shame?
- Have you seen your father or mother as a burden?
- Have you ignored or abandoned your father or mother?
- Do you fail to call or visit your father or mother?
- Are you ungrateful towards your father or mother?
- Have you stolen from your father or mother? (Cash or household goods)
- Have you misused your father or mother's checks, credit cards, or bank accounts?
- Have you financially exploited your father or mother?

Take time to reflect and ask the LORD to bring to memory those things you have done to dishonor your parents. Use the space below to journal everything HOLY SPIRIT reveals to you.

_____

_____

_____

_____

Prayer for Youth

Heavenly FATHER,

I ask forgiveness for every sin I have in my heart. I ask forgiveness for any resentment, bitterness, or lack of forgiveness I have towards my father and/or mother. I ask forgiveness for breaking Your fifth commandment. I ask forgiveness for not honoring my father and mother in a way that is pleasing to you. I ask forgiveness for every sin I have committed against my parents. (Name each one as HOLY SPIRIT guides you.) JESUS, I want You to become LORD of my life and my family. Restore my relationship with my parents. From this day forward I chose to honor my father and my mother. In JESUS's name, I pray. Amen!

The following is a list of spirits that may be in operation, hindering you from honoring your parents. Circle all that pertains to you. There may be other spirits as well, ask HOLY SPIRIT to reveal any that may not be listed.

- Spirit of bitterness
- Spirit of unforgiveness
- Spirit of hatred
- Spirit of resentment
- Spirit of insecurity
- Spirit of anger
- Spirit of rebellion
- Spirit of mockery
- Spirit of manipulation
- Spirit of stubbornness
- Spirit of lying
- Spirit of sarcasm
- Spirit of cruelty

Heavenly FATHER,

I renounce every evil that binds me, and I call upon You LORD JESUS to set me free. I renounce every demonic stronghold that stops me from honoring my parents. I renounce the spirit of _____. (Name each spirit separately.)

I bind the spirit of _____ and rebuke it out of my life. I order it out, never to return in the name of JESUS. (Repeat this with every spirit that has you bound.)

I go back four generations and in the name of JESUS, I break the power of any curse off myself and my generations because of my ancestors dishonoring their parents.

I close every door I have opened through the breaking of the fifth commandment. Satan, I break your powers off my life and my generations to come in Jesus's name I pray.

Lord, fill me with unconditional love for my parents. Fill me with humility and submission so I can walk in obedience. Show me ways I can honor my parents. I want to have a blessed relationship with my parents. In Jesus's name, I pray. Amen!

Prayer for Dishonoring an Elderly Parent

Heavenly Father,

I ask forgiveness for every sin I have in my heart. I ask forgiveness for any resentment, bitterness, or lack of forgiveness I have towards my father and/or mother. I ask forgiveness for mistreating them, for neglecting their needs, and not honoring them according to Your Word. I ask forgiveness for every sin I have committed against my parents. (Name each one as Holy Spirit guides you.) I ask you Lord to restore my relationship with my parents. From this day forward I chose to honor my father and my mother. In Jesus's name, I pray. Amen!

The following is a list of spirits that may be in operation, hindering you from honoring your elderly parents. Circle all that pertains to you. There may be other spirits as well, ask Holy Spirit to reveal any that may not be listed.

- Spirit of bitterness
- Spirit of unforgiveness
- Spirit of hatred
- Spirit of resentment
- Spirit of anger
- Spirit of insecurity
- Spirit of abuse (physical, verbal, sexual)
- Spirit of neglect
- Spirit of cruelty
- Spirit of exploitation
- Spirit of deception
- Spirit of selfishness

Heavenly FATHER,

I renounce every demonic stronghold that hinders me from honoring my elderly father/mother and I call upon You LORD JESUS to set me free. I renounce the spirit of _____. (Name each spirit separately.)

I bind the spirit of _____ and rebuke it out of my life. I order it out, never to return in the name of JESUS. (Repeat this with every spirit that has you bound.)

I go back four generations and in the name of JESUS, I break the power of any curse off myself and my generations because of my ancestors dishonoring their parents.

I close every door I have opened through the breaking of the fifth commandment. Satan, I break your powers off my life and my generations to come, in JESUS's name.

LORD, fill me with unconditional love for my parents. Fill me with gentleness and compassion so I can care for my elderly parents in a way that will bring honor to You. In JESUS's name, I pray. Amen!

Prayer for Parents

Heavenly FATHER,

I ask forgiveness for every sin I have in my heart. I ask forgiveness for neglecting my responsibilities as a parent to raise my child(ren) in a loving, nurturing way. I ask forgiveness for not demonstrating a godly lifestyle for my children. I ask forgiveness for _____. (Confess each sin HOLY SPIRIT reveals to you.) I ask forgiveness for seeing my children as an inconvenience and not seeing them as a blessing. I want to be the godly example my children need. Restore and heal my relationship with my children. In JESUS's name, I pray. Amen!

The following is a list of spirits that may be in operation, hindering you from treating your children correctly. Circle all that pertains to you. There may be other spirits as well, ask HOLY SPIRIT to reveal any that may not be listed.

- Spirit of abandonment

- Spirit of desertion
- Spirit of cruelty
- Spirit of anger
- Spirit of neglect
- Spirit of violence
- Spirit of abuse (physical, verbal, sexual)

Heavenly FATHER,

I renounce every demonic stronghold that influenced me to neglect and abuse my child(ren) and I call upon You LORD JESUS to set me free. I renounce the spirit of _____. (Name each spirit separately.)

I bind the spirit of _____ and rebuke it out of my life. I order it out, never to return in the name of JESUS. (Repeat this with every spirit that has you bound.)

I go back four generations and in the name of JESUS, I break the power of any curse off myself and my generations because of abuse in my ancestral linage.

I close every door I have opened through the breaking of the fifth commandment. Satan, I break your powers off my life and my generations to come, in JESUS's name I pray.

LORD, I know you have blessings for me and my family. Restore my relationship with my child(ren). Fill me with unconditional love. Fill me with gentleness and compassion so I can care for them in a way that will bring honor to You. I ask You HOLY SPIRIT to give me wisdom in training up my child(ren) in the ways of the LORD. Help me to be more Christ-like. In JESUS's name, I pray. Amen!

Once you have finished praying ask the LORD to show you if there is anything you need to do to restore His heart.

Return to Section 2 and begin reading *Chapter 13 – How Is Your Anger?*

Chapter 23
SIXTH COMMANDMENT

The following is a list of questions that will help determine if you have violated the sixth commandment. Identify the ones that apply to you.

- Have you murdered someone or wished someone were dead?
- Have you ever cursed yourself by saying "I wish I were dead"?
- Have you ever had an abortion?
- Have you ever attempted to commit suicide?
- Have you ever assisted someone to commit suicide?
- Do you have emotions of anger, bitterness, resentment, jealousy that are destroying your relationship with others?
- Have you slandered another person?
- Have you participated in gossip?
- Have you ever bullied anyone?
- Have you ever abused anyone? (physically, emotionally, psychologically, sexually)
- Do you have addictions that are destroying your body? (drugs, alcoholism, tobacco, gluttony)

Take time to reflect and ask the LORD to bring to memory those things you have done to offend Him through breaking the sixth commandment. Use the space provided on the next page to journal everything HOLY SPIRIT reveals to you.

_____

_____

_____

_____

Heavenly FATHER,

I ask forgiveness for breaking Your sixth commandment. Forgive me for my anger, resentment, bitterness, and speaking harsh words about others. I ask forgiveness for participating in gossip and speaking negatively about another individual. I ask forgiveness for any hatred I have in my heart (towards yourself and others). I ask forgiveness for any curse I have placed on my life or the life of others through words I have spoken. I ask forgiveness for any thoughts of suicide or murder. I ask forgiveness for thoughts of having an abortion or following through with an abortion. I ask forgiveness for not taking care of my temple in a healthy manner. I know it is only through the blood of JESUS that I can be set free from those things that hold me back from obeying Your sixth commandment. In JESUS's name, I pray. Amen!

The following is a list of spirits that may be in operation, hindering you from enjoying life and the life of others. Circle all that pertains to you. There may be other spirits as well, ask HOLY SPIRIT to reveal any that may not be listed.

- Spirit of unforgiveness
- Spirit of anger
- Spirit of bitterness
- Spirit of resentment
- Spirit of hatred
- Spirit of revenge
- Spirit of envy
- Spirit of jealousy
- Spirit of depression
- Spirit of self-destruction
- Spirit of destruction

- Spirit of murder
- Spirit of death
- Spirit of gossip
- Spirit of defamation (Slander, libel)
- Spirit of suicide
- Spirit of addiction
- Spirit of gluttony

Heavenly FATHER,

I renounce every demonic stronghold that hinders me from obeying Your sixth commandment and I call upon You LORD JESUS to set me free. I renounce the spirit of _____. (Name each one separately.)

I bind the spirit of _____ and rebuke it out of my life. I order it out, never to return in the name of JESUS. (Repeat this with every spirit that has you bound.)

I cancel every curse of death I have spoken over _____. (names, including yourself) I cancel the words of _____ that have placed a curse over _____'s life. (name each person)

I go back four generations and in the name of JESUS, I break the power of any curse off myself and my generations because of murder in my ancestral linage.

I close every door I have opened through the breaking of the sixth commandment. Satan, I break your powers off my life, off my children, my grandchildren, and my great-grandchildren in JESUS's name.

LORD, I want to speak blessings over those you have put in my path. Fill me with the fruit of Your SPIRIT. Fill me with unconditional love for myself and others. Help me to see myself and others as YOU see us. In JESUS's name, I pray. Amen!

Once you have finished praying ask the LORD to show you if there is anything you need to do to restore His heart.

Return to Section 2 and begin reading *Chapter 16 – Are You in Covenant?*

Chapter 24
SEVENTH COMMANDMENT

The following is a list of questions that will help determine if you have violated the seventh commandment. Identify the ones that apply to you.

- Have you had sexual relationships outside of marriage?
- Have you cheated on your spouse?
- Have you looked at pornography?
- Have you watched X-rated movies, DVDs, or videos with sexual content?
- Have you read books with sexploitation?
- Have you watched soap operas?
- Have you ever masturbated yourself?
- Have you ever engaged in any orgies?
- Have you ever had sex with an animal? (bestiality)
- Have you ever had anal sex? (sodomy)
- Have you ever engaged in cybersex?
- Have you ever participated in joke-telling or listening to jokes which contain sexual innuendoes?
- Have you made sexual gestures?
- Have you ever committed incest? (Sex with a relative)
- Have you ever raped anyone?
- Have you ever dressed in a sensuous way?
- Have you engaged in prostitution?
- Have you ever cross-dressed?
- Have you ever used sex toys to stimulate you sexually?

Take time to reflect and ask the LORD to bring to memory those things you have done to offend Him through breaking the seventh commandment. Ask Him to reveal any toxic thoughts you may have forgotten about. Use this space to journal everything HOLY SPIRIT reveals to you.

_____
_____
_____
_____

Heavenly FATHER,

I ask forgiveness for breaking Your seventh commandment. I ask forgiveness for every sexual activity that was outside of the covenant of marriage. I ask forgiveness for the sin of _____. (Name each one). I ask forgiveness for every impure thought. I know it is only through the blood of JESUS that I can be set free. In JESUS's name, I pray. Amen!

The following is a list of spirits that may be in operation, hindering you from walking in holiness and covenant with GOD and your spouse. Circle all that pertains to you. There may be other spirits as well, ask HOLY SPIRIT to reveal any that may not be listed.

- Sexual addiction
- Spirit of adultery
- Spirit of bestiality
- Spirit of death (through abortions)
- Sexual fantasies
- Spirit of flirting
- Spirit of fornication
- Spirit of idolatry
- Spirit of infidelity
- Spirit of incest
- Spirit of incubus/succubus
- Spirit of homosexuality
- Spirit of Jezebel

- Spirit of lesbianism
- Spirit of lust
- Spirit of masturbation
- Spirit of pedophilia
- Spirit of pornography
- Spirit of perversion
- Spirit of promiscuity
- Spirit of prostitution
- Spirit of seduction
- Spirit of sensuality
- Spirit of sodomy (anal sex)
- Spirit of transvestitism
- Spirit of unfaithfulness

Heavenly FATHER,

I renounce every demonic stronghold that stops me from obeying Your seventh commandment. I renounce any blood covenant I have established through sexual immorality with _____ (name each person) and cancel them in the name of JESUS. I renounce any covenant of death established through having an abortion. I renounce every sexual fantasy in the name of JESUS. I renounce the spirit of _____. (Name each one that pertains to you.)

I bind the spirit of _____ and rebuke it out of my life. I order it out, never to return in the name of JESUS. (Repeat this with every spirit that has you bound.)

I go back four generations and in the name of JESUS, I break the power of any curse off myself and my generations because of my ancestors committing sexual impurity.

I close every door I have opened through the breaking of the seventh commandment. Satan, I break your powers off my life, off my children, my grandchildren, and my great-grandchildren. I declare freedom in the name of JESUS.

LORD, I want to be in covenant with you. I apply the blood of JESUS over my mind, my eyes, and my ears. I ask you LORD to put a garment of holiness over my life. Fill me with purity so I can walk in covenant with You and with my spouse/future spouse so I can receive blessings for my life. In Jesus's name, I pray. Amen!

Once you have finished praying ask the Lord to show you if there is anything you need to do to restore His heart and those you have offended.

One last step in your deliverance, destroy all pornography material and any romance novels that would cause you to have sexual fanaticism or arousal.

Return to Section 2 and begin reading *Chapter 15 – Are You Sure It's Yours?*

Chapter 25
EIGHTH COMMANDMENT

The following is a list of questions that will help determine if you have violated the eighth commandment. Identify the ones that apply to you.

- Are you giving ten percent of your paycheck to the LORD?
- Are you giving to the LORD with a cheerful heart?
- Have you ever bought a lottery or raffle ticket?
- Have you ever played slot machines?
- Have you ever played card games or bingo for money?
- Have you ever bet on races? (horse, dog)
- Have you ever bet on a sports game?
- Have you ever worked and not claimed your income on your tax return?
- Have you falsified information by claiming deductions that were not true?
- Have you faked or exaggerated an illness or injury to obtain disability, workers' compensation or claims on automobile accident insurance?
- Were you legally receiving disability or workers' compensation pay and not report a change in your condition?
- Have you taken advantage of the welfare system? Did your monthly income increase, and you not report it?
- Have you hired someone to do a job for you and not pay them a fair salary for their work?
- Do you claim personal charges as company expenses?

- Have you ever written a check, knowing the funds were not available?
- Have you borrowed from someone and not returned what you promised?
- Have you broken something you borrowed and not offered to replace it?
- Do you habitually come to work late or leave early?
- Do you take excessive breaks or longer breaks than what you are supposed to?
- Have you given your best when working on the job?
- Have you ever embezzled money from your employer?
- Do you socialize during company time?
- Have you made personal copies or printed articles at the company's expense?
- Have you walked off with company pens, pencils, etc., and not return them?
- Have you ever shoplifted?
- Have you switched price tags on an item to pay less for it?
- Working as a cashier, have you ever stolen from the cash register?
- Have you ever opened food items, eaten them, and not paid for them?
- Have you ever gotten refills of a fountain drink when free refills were forbidden?
- Have you ever taken towels or other items from a hotel for a souvenir?
- Have you ever taken condiments from a restaurant for personal use at home?
- Were you ever undercharged at a restaurant and not bring it to the attention of your waitress or waiter?
- Have you ever noticed a mistake in your favor on a cash register receipt and not report it to the store?
- Have you ever stolen from another individual?
- Have you made or received illegal copies of CDs, DVDs, or software programs?
- Have you ever cheated on a test?

- Have you ever used someone else's work and claimed it as your own?
- Have you ever found something, and when the owner comes looking for it, not return it?

Take time to reflect and ask the LORD to bring to memory those things you have done to offend Him through breaking the eighth commandment. Journal below your thoughts.

_____

_____

_____

_____

Heavenly FATHER,

I ask forgiveness for breaking Your eighth commandment. Forgive me for robbing You of your tithe. Forgive me for my greed and stealing from others. I ask forgiveness for _____ (any sin HOLY SPIRIT brings to remembrance). Forgive me for my laziness and not giving my best to my employer. I know it is only through the blood of JESUS that I can be set free from these things. In JESUS's name, I pray. Amen!

The following is a list of spirits that may be in operation that is causing you to steal from others. Circle all that pertains to you. There may be other spirits as well, ask HOLY SPIRIT to reveal any that may not be listed.

- Spirit of exploitation
- Spirit of deception
- Spirit of usury
- Spirit of kleptomania
- Spirit of corruption
- Spirit of piracy
- Spirit of lying
- Spirit of greed
- Spirit of robbery
- Spirit of fraud

- Spirit of violence
- Spirit of mammon

Prayer

Heavenly FATHER,

I renounce every demonic stronghold that stops me from obeying Your eighth commandment and I call upon You LORD JESUS to set me free. I renounce the spirit of _____. (Name each one that pertains to you.)

I bind the spirit of _____ and rebuke it out of my life. I order it out, never to return in the name of JESUS. (Repeat this with every spirit that has you bound.)

I go back four generations and in the name of JESUS, I break the power of any curse off myself and my generations because of my ancestors committing exploitation, usury, fraud, or deception.

I close every door I have opened through the breaking of the eighth commandment. Satan, I break your powers off my life, off my children, my grandchildren, and my great-grandchildren in the name of JESUS.

LORD fill me with integrity. Help me to be content with what YOU have blessed me with. I want to give of my tithe as a form of worship to YOU. I choose to put my trust in YOU. In JESUS's name, I pray. Amen!

Making Restitution

GOD is a GOD of restitution. As you go through the steps of deliverance, keep in mind repentance is not enough. If your repentance is genuine, there will be a desire in your heart to make things right and restore those you have stolen from. There are scriptural guidelines to follow when pursuing restitution. First, go and confess to the individual you offended.

> *"Therefore, if you bring your gift to the altar, and there remember that your brother has something against you, leave your gift there before the altar, and go your way.*

231

First, be reconciled to your brother, and then come and offer your gift."

- Matthew 5:23-24

The general rule for restitution is to add 20% to the restored value of the stolen item.

And the LORD spoke to Moses, saying: "If a person sins and commits a trespass against the LORD by lying to his neighbor about what was delivered to him for safekeeping, or about a pledge, or a robbery, or if he has extorted from his neighbor, or if he has found what was lost and lies concerning it, and swears falsely — in any one of these things that a man may do in which he sins; then it shall be, because he has sinned and is guilty, that he shall restore what he has stolen, or the thing which he has extorted, or what was delivered to him for safekeeping, or the lost thing which he found, or all that about which he has sworn falsely. He shall restore its full value, add one-fifth more to it, and give it to whomever it belongs, on the day of his trespass offering."

- Leviticus 6:1-5

If you have no way of restoring the person you offended or one of his relatives, then you must present the restitution to the LORD.

"Speak to the children of Israel: When a man or woman commits any sin that men commit in unfaithfulness against the LORD, and that person is guilty, then he shall confess the sin which he has committed. He shall make restitution for his trespass in full, plus one-fifth of it, and give it to the one he has wronged. But if the man has no relative to whom restitution may be made for the wrong, the restitution for the wrong must go to the LORD for the priest, in addition to the ram of the atonement with which atonement is made for him."

- Numbers 5:6-8

The conversion of Zacchaeus is a prime example of true repentance (Luke 19:2-10). When Zacchaeus had an encounter, it brought conviction of sin and he recognized he had to restore those he stole from.

> *Then Zacchaeus stood and said to the* LORD, *"Look,* LORD, *I give half of my goods to the poor; and if I have taken anything from anyone by false accusation, I restore fourfold."*
> *- Luke 19:8*

From his actions, JESUS knew true repentance was in the heart of Zacchaeus.

Return to Section 2 and begin reading *Chapter 16 – What Web Are You Making?*

Chapter 26
NINTH COMMANDMENT

The following is a list of questions that will help determine if you have violated the ninth commandment. Identify the ones that apply to you.

- Do you compliment people when you don't mean it?
- Do you ask a family member to tell lies for you?
- Do you tell lies to keep yourself out of trouble?
- Do you tell creditors that "the check is in the mail" when you have not yet mailed it?
- Do you exaggerate when telling a story about yourself?
- Have you ever called off sick just to stay home when you were not sick?
- Have you spoken any "little white lies"?
- Have you used flattery to get your way?
- Have you made a false self-impression to others?
- Have you spoken badly about anyone?
- Have you spread or listened to rumors?
- Do you love to gossip?
- Have you ever spoken evil about another individual?
- Have you ever spoken words to ruin the reputation of another individual?
- Have you ever spoken a half-truth or remained quiet to make yourself or another individual appear innocent?
- Have you ever spoken falsely about anyone?
- Were you ever quick to judge someone?
- Have you made a promise that you did not fulfill?

Take time to reflect and ask the LORD to bring to memory those things you have done to offend Him through breaking the ninth commandment. Ask HOLY SPIRIT to reveal to you any promises you have made but have not yet fulfilled. Journal below your thoughts.

_____

_____

_____

Heavenly FATHER,

I ask forgiveness for every sin I have in my heart. I ask forgiveness for breaking your ninth commandment. Forgive me for every idle word that I have spoken. Forgive me for not controlling the words that have come out of my mouth. Forgive me for promises I have made and did not fulfill. Forgive me for the times I have talked about others behind their backs. Forgive me for not owning up to my mistakes, but rather keeping silent. I ask forgiveness for the times I have exaggerated to draw attention to myself. Forgive me for being quick to judge others. I repent of every sin I have committed through breaking your ninth commandment. In the name of JESUS, I pray. Amen!

The following is a list of spirits that may be in operation, hindering you from walking in integrity. Circle all that pertains to you. There may be other spirits as well, ask HOLY SPIRIT to reveal any that may not be listed.

- Spirit of pride
- Spirit of fear
- Spirit of lying
- Spirit of deception
- Spirit of exaggeration
- Spirit of flattery
- Spirit of slander
- Spirit of false accusation
- Spirit of error
- Spirit of hypocrisy

- Promise breaking spirit
- Spirit of gossip
- Critical spirit
- Spirit of belittling
- Spirit of spite
- Judgmental spirit

Prayer

Heavenly FATHER,

I renounce every demonic stronghold that stops me from obeying Your ninth commandment I renounce the spirit of _____. (Name each one that pertains to you.)

I bind the spirit of _____ and rebuke it out of my life. I order it out, never to return in the name of JESUS. (Repeat this with every spirit that has you bound.)

I go back four generations and in the name of JESUS, I break the power of any curse off myself and my generations because of my ancestors not walking with integrity.

I close every door I have opened through the breaking of the ninth commandment. Satan, I break your powers off my life, over my children, my grandchildren, and my great-grandchildren in JESUS's name.

I recognize I cannot control my tongue on my own, so I order my tongue to come under submission to HOLY SPIRIT. HOLY SPIRIT brings conviction to my spirit when I say things I ought not to speak. Help me to control my tongue so I do not break the ninth commandment any longer. Fill me with a spirit of truth so my actions and words will be with integrity. In JESUS's name, I pray. Amen!

Once you have finished praying ask the LORD to show you if there is anything you need to do to restore His heart. If you have made any promises that have not yet been fulfilled, go to that person, ask forgiveness, and make right your commitment to that individual.

Return to Section 2 and begin reading *Chapter 17 – What Do You Long For?*

Chapter 27

TENTH COMMANDMENT

The following is a list of questions that will help determine if you have violated the tenth commandment. Identify the ones that apply to you.

- Do you rob GOD of His tithe because of other debts?
- Do you invest more in material things rather than investing in GOD's kingdom?
- Do you covet things that others have?
- Do you become jealous when others have what you do not?
- Do you always want the newest version of technology?
- Are your total bills each month greater than you're your total income each month?
- Are you stingy with your money?
- Would you rather sell items you no longer want than to give them to those in need?
- When you see something you want, do you buy it on impulse?
- Is more of your spending because of your wants rather than your needs?
- Is your goal in life to become rich?
- Do you try to outdo your neighbor?
- Do you go shopping when you are depressed?
- Do you look for material things to bring you happiness?
- Do you resist when HOLY SPIRIT prompts your heart to give?

- Does your giving have a motive behind it?
- Do you see GOD as an ATM when you give?

For those in ministry
- Does your preaching focus mainly on prosperity or do you confront sin?
- Has the focus of your ministry been on the size of your congregation rather than the condition of the souls?
- Have you used the Word of GOD to manipulate people into giving?

Take time to reflect and ask the LORD to bring to memory those things you have done to offend Him through breaking the tenth commandment. Journal below your thoughts.

_____
_____
_____
_____

Heavenly FATHER,

I ask forgiveness for every sin I have in my heart. I ask forgiveness for breaking Your tenth commandment. Forgive me for coveting material things and wanting the best of technology. I ask forgiveness for the times I robbed you of your tithe. If I have been hesitant when you have prompted me to give, I ask your forgiveness. I ask forgiveness for being self-centered rather than thinking of others. I ask forgiveness for envying others and becoming jealous when others have what I do not have. Forgive me for spending beyond my financial means. Forgive me for my greed for material things. Forgive me if my giving was with wrong motives or gave less than what you asked me to give. I want my focus to be on my eternal inheritance, not on earthly gains. I ask You HOLY SPIRIT to show me every demonic stronghold that keeps me bound and prompts me to sin against Your tenth commandment. In the name of JESUS, I pray.

The following is a list of spirits that may be in operation causing you to covet. Circle all that pertains to you. There may be other spirits as well, ask HOLY SPIRIT to reveal any that may not be listed.

- Spirit of selfishness
- Spirit of arrogance
- Spirit of jealousy
- Spirit of envy
- Spirit of greed
- Spirit of pride
- Spirit of lust
- Spirit of obsession
- Spirit of vanity
- Spirit of mammon
- Spirit of self-centeredness
- Spirit of egotism
- Spirit of disillusionment
- Spirit of stinginess

Prayer

Heavenly FATHER,

I renounce every demonic stronghold that hinders me from obeying Your tenth commandment and I call upon You LORD JESUS to set me free. I renounce the spirit of _____. (Name each one separately.)

I bind the spirit of _____ and rebuke it out of my life. I order it out, never to return in the name of JESUS. (Repeat this with every spirit that has you bound.)

I go back four generations and in the name of JESUS, I break the power of any curse off myself and my generations because of any covetousness my ancestors had.

I close every door I have opened through the breaking of the tenth commandment. Satan, in the name of JESUS, I break your powers off my life, off my children, my grandchildren, and my great-grandchildren.

LORD fill me with a spirit of contentment. Fill me with joy when I see Your blessings fall on other individuals. Fill me with humility so when prosperity comes, I do not become proud. Fill me with a giving heart so I can be a blessing to others. In JESUS's name, I pray. Amen!

Once you have finished praying ask the LORD to show you if there is anything you need to do to restore His heart.

I trust you have completed each section of your deliverance process and have begun to enjoy the freedom GOD has for your life. Be sure to read the epilogue for some final instructions.

EPILOGUE

There is a tremendous battle going on in the spiritual realm for your soul. You cannot discredit the reality of Satan and the influence he can have on your life. The adversary will not give up easily, he loves to see GOD's people defeated. But you don't have to walk in defeat. You have the power to overcome sin and cancel curses off your life through the precious blood of JESUS. Now that you have a better understanding of how you can offend the heart of GOD and unnoticeably open doors to curses upon your life, be vigilant to the tactics of the adversary. He is roaming around like a roaring lion, seeking whom he may devour. Don't let it be you. Take the necessary actions to make certain you do not fall prey again. *Your Ultimate Freedom-Hidden Curses Revealed* has given you the basic steps to overcome the bondage of sin. Utilize them and receive your ultimate freedom.

Nurture your relationship with GOD. Surrender your heart totally and enjoy your love covenant with Him. If you have followed the instructions provided in this book, you have closed the open doors and canceled the legal rights the adversary had over you. Draw close to GOD and enjoy a fruitful relationship with HOLY SPIRIT. Remember this is just the beginning of a life-long process. You have a responsibility in maintaining your deliverance. Seek HOLY SPIRIT and read GOD's Word daily. Worship GOD in spirit and truth and seek ways to serve Him.

Are you ready to continue your journey with the LORD? He has new things for your life and promises from His Word to fulfill in and through you. The best is yet to come as you walk in blessings and enjoy your ultimate freedom. Be blessed, be free, and Shalom!

ABOUT THE AUTHOR

Pamela Wood is a faithful member and leader of ABBA Ministries in Kissimmee, Florida. She flows in the prophetic and has over twenty years of experience in the deliverance ministry on an individual, city, and state level. The testimonies of healing and deliverance that occurred in her life affirm that the ministry of YESHUA is the same yesterday, today, and forevermore. Her passion is to see the bondage of sin and curses broken off the lives of believers so they can walk in ultimate freedom and in the blessings and divine purposes GOD has for their lives.

NOTES

Why Do I Struggle?

[1]Strong, J. (1995). The new Strong's exhaustive concordance of the Bible: with main concordance, appendix to the main concordance, topical index to the Bible, dictionary of the Hebrew Bible, dictionary of the Greek Testament (p. 13). T. Nelson Publishers. Greek Reference 726

[2]Strong, J. (1995). The new Strong's exhaustive concordance of the Bible: with main concordance, appendix to the main concordance, topical index to the Bible, dictionary of the Hebrew Bible, dictionary of the Greek Testament (p. 45). T. Nelson Publishers. Greek Reference 2588

[3]How Anger Affects Your Heart: Allegiance Health - A regional hospital and health system located in Jackson, Michigan. (2013, January 29). Retrieved December 3, 2016, from http://www.allegiancehealth.org/blog/heart/how-anger-affects-your-heart

How Can I Obtain My Freedom?

[1]Definition of REPENT. (n.d.). www.Merriam-Webster.com. Retrieved January 4, 2020, from http://www.merriam-webster.com/dictionary/repent

[2]Definition of RENOUNCE. (n.d.). www.Merriam-Webster.Com. Retrieved January 4, 2020, from http://www.merriam-webster.com/dictionary/renounce

Law or No Law

[1]Strong, J. (1995). The new Strong's exhaustive concordance of the Bible: with main concordance, appendix to the main concordance, topical index to the Bible, dictionary of the Hebrew Bible, dictionary of the Greek Testament (p. 72). T. Nelson Publishers. Greek Reference 4137

[2]Strong, J. (1995). The new Strong's exhaustive concordance of the Bible: with main concordance, appendix to the main concordance, topical index to the Bible, dictionary of the Hebrew Bible, dictionary of the Greek Testament (p. 19). T. Nelson Publishers. Greek Reference 1096

Religion or Relationship?
[1]Definition of COVENANT. (n.d.). www.Merriam-Webster.com. Retrieved February 12, 2020, from http://www.merriam-webster.com/dictionary/covenant

The Weight Is Off, Now What?
[1]Strong, J. (1995). The new Strong's exhaustive concordance of the Bible: with main concordance, appendix to the main concordance, topical index to the Bible, dictionary of the Hebrew Bible, dictionary of the Greek Testament (p. 84). T. Nelson Publishers. Hebrew Reference 4714

[2]Strong, J. (1995). The new Strong's exhaustive concordance of the Bible: with main concordance, appendix to the main concordance, topical index to the Bible, dictionary of the Hebrew Bible, dictionary of the Greek Testament (p. 101). T. Nelson Publishers. Hebrew Reference 5647

Why Do I Feel So Oppressed?
[1]Definition of OCCULT. (n.d.). www.Merriam-Webster.com. Retrieved March 6, 2020, from http://www.merriam-webster.com/dictionary/occult

[2]Keohane, S. (n.d.). Christians Beware - of Freemasonry. Bibleprobe.Com. Retrieved April 28, 2020, from http://bibleprobe.com/freemasonry.htm

[3]Schnoebelen, W. (1991). Masonry: Beyond the light (2nd ed., p. 212). Chick Publ.

[4]Schnoebelen, W. (1991). Masonry: Beyond the light (2nd ed., p. 87-88). Chick Publ.

[5]Wilson, E. (n.d.). The Secrets Behind Martial Arts! The Secrets Behind Martial Arts! Retrieved May 1, 2020, from https://secretdangersofmartialarts.wordpress.com/

Notes

[6]Knight, J., Schilling, C., Barnett, A., Jackson, R., & Clarke, P. (2016). Revisiting the "Christmas Holiday Effect" in the Southern Hemisphere. Journal of the American Heart Association: Cardiovascular and Cerebrovascular Disease, 5(12). https://doi.org/10.1161/JAHA.116.005098

Are You Guilty?

[1]Definition of VAIN. (n.d.). www.Merriam-Webster.com. Retrieved May 7, 2020, from http://www.merriam-webster.com/dictionary/vain

Have You Taken Your Break?

[1]Strong, J. (1995). The new Strong's exhaustive concordance of the Bible: with main concordance, appendix to the main concordance, topical index to the Bible, dictionary of the Hebrew Bible, dictionary of the Greek Testament (p. 137). T. Nelson Publishers. Hebrew Reference 7676

How Can I With So Much Pain?

[1]Salleh, M. R. (2008). Life Event, Stress and Illness. The Malaysian Journal of Medical Sciences: MJMS, 15(4), 9–18. https://www.ncbi.nlm.nih.gov/pmc/articles/PMC3341916

[2]Strong, J. (1995). The new Strong's exhaustive concordance of the Bible: with main concordance, appendix to the main concordance, topical index to the Bible, dictionary of the Hebrew Bible, dictionary of the Greek Testament (p. 62). T. Nelson Publishers. Hebrew Reference 3513

[3]Strong, J. (1995). The new Strong's exhaustive concordance of the Bible: with main concordance, appendix to the main concordance, topical index to the Bible, dictionary of the Hebrew Bible, dictionary of the Greek Testament (p. 90). T. Nelson Publishers. Greek Reference 5091.

[4]Strong, J. (1995). The new Strong's exhaustive concordance of the Bible: with main concordance, appendix to the main concordance, topical index to the Bible, dictionary of the Hebrew Bible, dictionary of the Greek Testament (p. 94). T. Nelson Publishers. Greek Reference 5293

[5]Strong, J. (1995). The new Strong's exhaustive concordance of the Bible: with main concordance, appendix to the main concordance, topical index to the Bible, dictionary of the Hebrew Bible, dictionary of the Greek Testament (p. 140). T. Nelson Publishers. Hebrew Reference 7843

[6]Elder Abuse Statistics & Facts | Elder Justice | NCOA. (2018, June 18). NCOA. https://www.ncoa.org/public-policy-action/elder-justice/elder-abuse-facts/

How Is Your Anger?
[1]Strong, J. (1995). The new Strong's exhaustive concordance of the Bible: with main concordance, appendix to the main concordance, topical index to the Bible, dictionary of the Hebrew Bible, dictionary of the Greek Testament (p. 134). Nashville, TN: Thomas Nelson. Hebrew Reference 7523

[2]Howard, J. (2019, June 18). *How to look for suicide warning signs*. CNN. https://www.cnn.com/2019/06/18/health/suicide-rates-teens-young-adults-us-study/index.html

[3]Holland, K. (2018, November). What Are the 12 Leading Causes of Death in the United States? Healthline; Healthline Media. https://www.healthline.com/health/leading-causes-of-death#worldwide-causes

Are You in Covenant?
[1]Definition of COVENANT. (n.d.). www.Merriam-Webster.com. Retrieved February 12, 2020, from http://www.merriam-webster.com/dictionary/covenant

[2]Strong, J. (1995). The new Strong's exhaustive concordance of the Bible: with main concordance, appendix to the main concordance, topical index to the Bible, dictionary of the Hebrew Bible, dictionary of the Greek Testament (p. 40). T. Nelson Publishers. Hebrew Reference 2319

[3]Strong, J. (1995). The new Strong's exhaustive concordance of the Bible: with main concordance, appendix to the main concordance, topical index to the Bible, dictionary of the Hebrew Bible, dictionary of the Greek Testament (p. 45). T. Nelson Publishers. Greek Reference 2537

Notes

[4]Basic Statistics. (2019). CDC: Centers for Disease Control and Prevention. https://www.cdc.gov/hiv/basics/statistics.html

[5]Holland, K. (n.d.). Sore Vagina After Sex: Causes, Symptoms, and Treatments for Pain. Healthline. Retrieved May 22, 2020, from https://www.healthline.com/health/sore-vagina-after-sex Medically reviewed by Janet Brito, Ph.D., LCSW, CST on September 23, 2019 —.

[6]Staff, C. N. (2014, October 7). Shocker: Study Shows Most Christian Men Are Into Porn. Charisma News. https://www.charismanews.com/us/45671-shocker-study-shows-most-christian-men-are-into-porn

[7]Questions and Concerns About Masturbation. (n.d.). Focus on the Family. Retrieved May 26, 2020, from https://www.focusonthefamily.com/family-qa/questions-and-concerns-about-masturbation/

Does it Belong to You?
[1]Brandon Gaille. (2017, May 25). 27 Jaw Dropping Employee Theft Statistics. BrandonGaille.Com. https://brandongaille.com/26-jaw-dropping-employee-theft-statistics/

[2]Definition of COPYRIGHT. (n.d.). www.Merriam-Webster.com. Retrieved June 1, 2020, from http://www.merriam-webster.com/dictionary/copyright

What Web Are You Making?
[1]Definition of EXAGGERATION. (n.d.). www.Merriam-Webster.Com. Retrieved June 1, 2020, from http://www.merriam-webster.com/dictionary/exaggeration

What Do You Long For?
[1]Definition of COVET. (n.d.). www.Merriam-Webster.com. Retrieved June 3, 2020, from http://www.merriam-webster.com/dictionary/covet

[2]Strong, J. (1995). The new Strong's exhaustive concordance of the Bible: with main concordance, appendix to the main concordance, topical index to the Bible, dictionary of the Hebrew Bible, dictionary

of the Greek Testament (p. 44). T. Nelson Publishers. Hebrew Reference 2530

Made in the USA
Columbia, SC
20 April 2023

15313722R00155